FINCURIOUS®

INDIA • SINGAPORE • MALAYSIA

Notion Press

No.8, 3rd Cross Street, CIT Colony,
Mylapore, Chennai,
Tamil Nadu – 600004

First Published by Notion Press 2020
Copyright © Rahul Saria 2020
All Rights Reserved.

ISBN 978-1-64899-989-5

STARTUP FINANCE

FINCURIOUS®

LET'S KEEP IT SIMPLE

BUSINESS, FUNDING AND STARTUPS
Foreword by Nilesh Vikamsey, Past President ICAI

RAHUL SARIA

INDIA · SINGAPORE · MALAYSIA

INDICACADEMY

INDIC PLEDGE

———❧❧———

- *I celebrate our civilisational identity, continuity & legacy in thought, word and deed.*

- *I believe our indigenous thought has solutions for the global challenges of health, happiness, peace, and sustainability.*

- *I shall seek to preserve, protect and promote this heritage in doing so,*
  - *discover, nurture and harness my potential,*
  - *connect, cooperate and collaborate with fellow seekers,*
  - *be inclusive and respectful of diverse opinions.*

ABOUT INDIC ACADEMY

———❧❧———

Indic Academy is a non-traditional 'university' for traditional knowledge. We seek to bring about a global renaissance based on Indic civilizational and indigenous thought. We are pursuing a multidimensional strategy across time, space and cause by establishing centers of excellence, transforming intellectuals and building an ecosystem.

Indic Academy is pleased to support this book.

OM SHRI GANESHAYA NAMAH!

BISMILLAH ~ بسملة!

IN THE NAME OF GOD!

SATNAM WAHEGURU!

Contents

Annexures

Foreword

I am happy that CA Rahul Saria based on his varied experience in the start-up space, has written a short self-help book on Startup Finance" which covers – How to start-up from an idea stage?, How to raise funds for the start up?, How to manage finance and legal aspects?, Knowledge on Investors and fund-raising process and covers more aspects of Start-ups financing.

Books are an amazing source of inspiration. Offering some insights into practical real-world tips, non-fiction books like this have always been a source of knowledge for entrepreneurs. Even the busiest of the successful entrepreneurs like Mark Zuckerberg and Bill Gates make sure that they cater some time daily for reading books. These non-fiction books make it easy to draw inspiration from some of the experienced and insightful in the industry. While entrepreneurship is not just about doing one specific task perfectly, it is a combination of a multitude of skills, knowledge and domain understanding. Since the required domain knowledge is hard to gain without gaining some entrepreneurial experience in one's niche, that void is filled by these types of books.

I am sure this book will be very useful to Start up Technocrats, Finance professionals looking at start-ups for career opportunities, students and others.

I extend my heartiest wishes and would like to congratulate Rahul for his publication of the book. He has done an excellent job of explaining a difficult concept based on his experience. I have nothing but admiration and respect for anyone having practical experience, who takes out time and puts pen to paper.

WISHING THE BOOK AND RAHUL A GRAND SUCCESS!

– CA Nilesh Vikamsey

Past President ICAI;
Director – SBI Life, IIFL,
Thomas Cook, PNB Housing, Navneet Publication etc.

Preface

Whether you are a beginner or a pro in business, this condensed self-help book will help you decipher the new age businesses and entrepreneurs from the scratch. This compilation is an output of a very deep and rich first-hand experience with multiple super successful, successful, unsuccessful and not so successful founders and CXOs across the country and of course the beloved Investors community.

The best way to read and gain from this book is to start on a clean slate with an open mind. Few parts may not be of much interest to the segment veterans, but the idea is to be helpful and reachable to as many as possible.

One can look up themselves for different topics and get familiarized, but the facts and the thoughts shared here will not be taught in any of the business school in its entirety. Neither can google help in such a structured manner, since one doesn't know what to search for and the right place to search. As they say, the best way to learn is to practice. This is a culmination of that experience, which can be very fruitful.

In this book, the focus has been on converting your idea into a startup and help your journey through the lens of legal and finance. Often, the founders who do not have finance expertise are caught up and get confused when it comes to finance and legal aspects of business. So, while you focus on your business, this would enhance your knowledge & confidence and shall answer a lot of questions that every entrepreneur seeks.

To get the best out of this compilation, don't hesitate to mark the texts, make notes and use the search engines to deep dive and know more on the topics/areas of your interest.

This book is relevant across the globe, except that the legal framework/ taxation laws have been referred to in Indian context. (It is advisable to refer to the local applicable laws).

They say some are Curios for knowledge, some are Incurious i.e. not eager to know something, lacking curiosity; but we are **Fincurious**® i.e. financially cu-rious.

Fincuriosly yours.

Happy Entrepreneurship and Financing!

Acknowledgments

I dedicate this book to my loving parents, Sri Debu Saria and Srimati Daya Saria. Whatever I am, is because of their blessings, love, guidance and support.

I acknowledge the support of my wife CA. Ansul Goyal, without whom this would have never seen the light of the day. Further, she helped me proof-read this book diligently.

I acknowledge the contribution of numerous entrepreneurs, founders, investors, CFOs, finance heads, my mentors, colleagues in my journey of learning and helping me all throughout.

A perpetual learner. Lots of Love!

– **Rahul**

Chapter 1

Finance - Terms & Jargons

The key to understanding start-up finance is being well accustomed to varied acronyms and financial jargons used in the industry. Generally, if you are a first-time entrepreneur or a non-finance background personnel, you would get perplexed on hearing the perpetual use of these terms around you.

The below given definitions & explanations are in a simple layman language which shall help break this taboo and ensure that the next time someone uses a jargon, you are not left walking away without a response or a challenging question in response.

Let's start with some very elementary terms (alphabetically) that may have become common in the startup space only in the last decade but generally misunderstood or loosely used. The best way to read this chapter is to take a quick glance and jump to the next. Further, as and when needed keep referring to the following definitions for a clearer and stronger understanding. However, if you find something interesting, do spend some time in grasping the same.

Interesting terms and jargons:

- **AIF (Alternative Investment Funds)** – The funds established or incorporated in India, which is a privately pooled investment vehicle. Many PEs/VCs are registered as an AIF. These are regulated as per SEBI regulations.

- **Angel Investors** – Initial Investors for smaller sizes of cheques, generally, HNIs (High Net worth Individuals)

- **Anti-Dilution Provision** – A provision in the Shareholders agreement (SHA). Also called, pre-emptive rights, subscription privileges, or subscription rights.

- **As if converted basis** – The Cap table drawn to show the percentage ownership in the company assuming all the convertible instruments (E.g. Convertible Preference shares, convertible Debentures) have been converted into Equity Shares. This does not include dilution instruments like ESOP pool. Also see Fully Diluted Cap table.

- **Basis Points (Bps)** – This means 1/100 or One-hundredth of one percentage point i.e. 100 Bps = 1%. Pronounced as Bips. Usually used in interest rate conversation. E.g. The interest rate has gone up by 10 Bps, which means, it has increased by 0.10%.

- **Beta Version** – a version of a piece of software that is made available for testing, typically by a limited number of users outside the company that is developing it, before its general release.

- **B2B** – Business to Business i.e. Selling of goods or provision of service to other business houses/companies etc. E.g. Udaan, Near.co

- **B2C** – Business to Consumer i.e. Selling of products or services to consumers directly e.g. Flipkart, Rentomojo.com

- **Cap Table/Capitalization table** – The table comprising of list of shareholders along with their shareholding in numbers as well percentage ownership. *Also see Fully Diluted Cap table.*

- **Cash Burn** – The Net cash outflow of the business, i.e. The cash outflow of expenses reduced by Revenue cash inflow, if any. Often, this is tracked as Monthly Cash burn.

- **Cohort** – A cohort is a group of data of common characteristics. E.g. Sales for the month of April and retention thereof in May and June vis-a-vis sales for May and retention thereof in June.

- **Customer Acquisition Cost (CAC)** – The marketing and sales cost spent on acquiring a customer/user i.e. spends on compelling a customer to purchase the product/avail the service.

- **CXO** – Chief/Top officers of the Company eg. CEO, COO, CFO, CRO, CTO etc.

- **Data Book** – A summary of financial and business performance for a particular period shared with prospective Investors. It may also be seen as a well-defined and structured MIS.

- **Data Room** – A folder which contains all the shareable data to a prospective Investor or the Due Diligence team

- **Debentures/Loan** – A Debt raised by the company and repayable with interest.

- **Definitive Agreements** – A document defining the final terms of an agreement between buyer and seller, typically of a company's assets or stock. e.g. SHA and SSA.

- **Dilution** – The percentage stake/shareholding that the new investor owns and the existing shareholders part away with.

- **Dilution Instruments** – Any Instrument which, if exercised would dilute the ownership percentage of the shareholders e.g. ESOPs, Convertible Debentures etc.

- **Due Diligence** – Due diligence is an investigation or audit of a potential investment or product to confirm all facts, that includes the review of financial records. It refers to the research done before entering into an agreement or a financial transaction with another party.

- **Early stage startup** – A young company typically in its early formative years (1–3 years), when it tries to test its product/offering and establish itself.

- **Equity Shares** – Equity shareholders are the owners of the company and the share certificate represent the ownership legally. Equity shares are those shares which are ordinary in the course of company's business. They are also called as ordinary shares. These shareholders do not enjoy preference regarding payment of dividend and repayment of capital. Equity shareholders are paid dividend out of the profits made by a company.

- **Financial Statements** – It consists of Balance Sheet, Profit & Loss Statement and Cash flow statement.

  - **Balance Sheet** – A statement of Assets and Liabilities drawn on a particular date, say 31st March.

  - **Profit and Loss Statement (P/L)** – A statement of Income and expenses for a particular period say one year.

  - **Cash flow Statement** – The cash receipts (Inflow) and cash pay-outs (Outflow) in the business.

- **Financial Year** – Generally in India, it is April to Mar (12 months period). It may differ in some geographies – e.g. July to June.

- **Founder/Co-founder** – The promoters of the company, who starts a business with a new idea.

- **Fully Diluted Cap table** – The table comprising of list of shareholders along with their shareholding in numbers as well percentage ownership on a fully diluted basis i.e. assuming all the convertible/dilution instruments are converted into Equity shares e.g. ESOPs, CCPS etc.

- **Funding rounds** – A Company raises money from various investors at different stages which are typically called as funding rounds. For example; Seed round, Venture Capitals (VC) round, Private Equity (PE) round, Series A, B, C…

- **Instruments/Financial Instrument** – The document representing the rights of the holder as an owner in the business/firm.

- **Investment Banker** – A professional who often works as a part of a financial institution and is primarily involved in raising capital for companies. These bankers are different regular commercial banks, where the customers open their bank accounts.

- **Life-Time Value (LTV) of a customer** – The potential earning that the company can make from a customer in its lifetime through its offering.

- **MIS** (Management Information system) – Financial and business reports prepared for the Management and the Investors to be shared periodically, usually, monthly or quarterly.

- **Minimum Viable Product (MVP)** – A MVP is a product with just enough features to satisfy early customers and provide feedback for future product development.

- **NBFC – Non-banking financial Company** – A financial institution that does not provide full banking services but are in lending/Investment business governed by the central bank i.e. RBI in India.

- **Preference Shares** – A share which entitles the holder to a fixed dividend, whose payment takes priority over that of ordinary share dividends. E.g. CCPS – Compulsory Convertible Preference Shares.

- **Private Equity (PE)** – Large funds houses with deep pockets who invest in late stage startups. They often write bigger cheques.

- **Projections** – The financial model of the company for the upcoming periods including revenue forecast, cost assumptions, business model etc.

- **Registrar of Companies (ROC)** – The government body under the Ministry of Corporate Affairs (MCA), which registers, manages and governs the Companies and LLPs.

- **Repeat Customer or Retention** – A customer or user opting to purchase or avail the service more than once.

- **Retention** – Measurement of number of repeat customers and the churn, represented in percentage or as a trend.

- **Runway** – The number of months (period) for which the company can survive without running out of cash. It is calculated by dividing the cash balance by the average (expected) monthly cash burn.

- **Sales Funnel** – A marketing term/concept showcasing the journey of a potential customer converting in an actual customer. E.g. Leads --> Sign ups --> Verified Sign Ups --> Customer

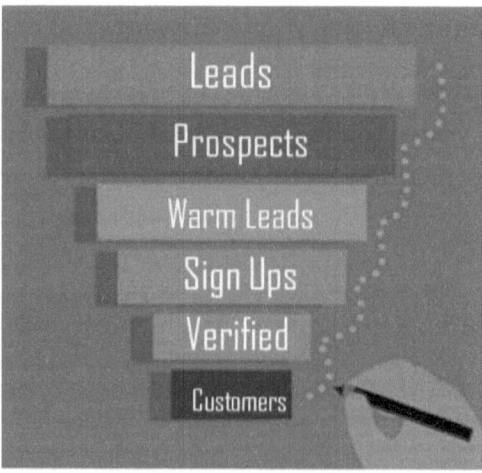

- **Share Subscription agreement (SSA)** – An agreement between the Company, promoters and the subscribing shareholder(s) in a particular round of funding i.e. the Investor who is buying new shares of the company.

- **Shareholders Agreement (SHA)** – An agreement among the shareholders (Founders, Investors etc.) and the Company on their rights, obligations, authorities, duties etc.

- **Traction** – A measurable set of customers, users, revenue, market share etc. that can validate the business as well can appeal to an Investor or catch and attract attention.

- **Transaction** – In terms of capital raising, raising of money in form of Debt or Equity from the Investors. Even Mergers & Acquisitions (M&A) are also termed as such.

- **Unit Economics** – The revenue, the variable or direct costs associated with a business model and the contribution margins expressed on a per unit basis.

- **Valuation** – The valuation of the company i.e. the worth of the company that its owners own.

  - **Pre-Money valuation** – The valuation before the cash investment raised in the said round of funding. The shareholding distribution is decided based on this valuation.

  - **Post-Money valuation** – The valuation post the cash Investment raised in a particular round of funding. E.g. A company raises $10M at a Pre Money valuation of $90M, thus the Post Money valuation is $100M.

- **Venture Capital (VC)** – Funds who Invest in early stage startups for a percentage stake in a company.

- **Venture Debt** – Loan provided by Venture debt firms to startups without collateral.

Chapter 2

Starting up

"If you don't build your own dream, someone else will hire you to build theirs"

– Dhirubhai Ambani, Founder, Reliance

A pertinent question that troubles every wannabe entrepreneur is taking the first step towards the risky zone. Moving from the comforts to the unknown risky territory. The ones who dare to do the same, definitely enjoy the fruits of the hard work. No wonder, why 90% of the wealth is held by 10% of the population. Yes, these 10% are the entrepreneurs, the risk takers. Though the road of entrepreneurship is not a cakewalk, but the fruits that it reaps makes it worth.

For starting up, what is that one thing or an attribute that would make up for the absence of everything else? Bingo, you are spot on, its' called PASSION *[Passion is a feeling of intense enthusiasm towards or compelling desire for someone or something. Passion can range from eager interest in or admiration for an idea, proposal, or cause; to enthusiastic enjoyment of an interest or activity; to strong attraction, excitement, or emotion towards a person.]* If you are not passionate enough for the business idea and its impact, it is next to impossible for the said idea to succeed. Only when you as an entrepreneur are ready to put in all your efforts with heart and soul, sacrificing all the material/trivial stuffs, rising up with more zeal every time you fall, will your enterprise see the light of the day.

While, passion is something that cannot be substituted, however, here are a few other drivers for one to self-start:

- Independence and freedom

  The 9 to 6 job always has a chip on your shoulder, it's time to throw that away and have ample time to plan, think and put your efforts in the right place. Entrepreneurship ensures independence of time with no legal (employer) obligation and no time commitment. With the time available, one can do multi-tasking.

- Ownership

  Be your own boss. This is the most important motivation for anyone to opt for entrepreneurship. Even if it is small, owning something gives a far larger satisfaction than working in a large MNC.

- Wealth creation

  The job can never promise create wealth for the next and the future generations. Owning your own business does. It gives us financial independency and freedom. It has been rightly coined, if you want to be wealthy, create your own equity.

The famous and one of the best-selling author Mr. Robert Kiyosaki in his book "Rich Dad Poor Dad" has made a very interesting comparison of an employer and an employee. The difference between an employee and the employer is that an employee earns salary, pays taxes (TDS) and spends what is left, whereas in case of the employer, they earn money, spend and debit expenses to their Profit and Loss Account, thereafter pay taxes on whatever is left i.e. the profits. It's a stark irony, nothing but the truth.

Employee Vs Corporation

Employee	Corporation
Earns Salary	Earns Income
Pays taxes (Tax deduction at source)	Spends – As it likes
Spends – If something is left	Pays Taxes – If something is left

And the employee is always seen working harder and harder.

Alas! the employer/bosses are seen playing golf, enjoying their life after the initial struggle.

For any founder, the biggest challenge is to take the first step, the only problem is that we are afraid to startup, it's similar to going to a gym, but once you hit the gym, the feeling is enormous and satisfying and one is motivated to keep going.

So. let's start. Go… Get Going… I strongly disagree with the famous idiom "Don't be a jack of all trades", and so does every wannabe entrepreneur, they need to wear multiple hats to run their business. Thus, I say, "Be a jack of all trades and master of ONE", it's always good to have a strong grip at least in one area.

While passion is THE thing, to have the courage to startup; there are various elements that you need to think about and work on for your dream idea:

a. Idea/Product

b. People (Team)

c. Customers/Target Group

d. Initial Capital

The idea or the product that you are developing needs a strong validation before offering to your customers. There are multiple questions that you should ask yourself from a customers' perspective like Why is this product great? Is this really solving a problem? Will the customers be willing to pay for it?

To get the answers to these, a Beta version i.e. a half-baked product can be tested in the market by offering the same to friends, families, general public and take feedback for product improvement and development. This is called Minimum Viable Product (MVP). At times, we as founders may think our idea is unique and one of the best, but the notion of being good should always be tested for its reality. Further, the founder should be aware of its competitors within the country as well globally who has developed same or similar products and their status.

Along with the initial validation, product market fit (PMF) is critical, it is the degree to which a product satisfies a strong market demand. This can be achieved by re-iterative process of development, testing, taking feedback and re-development. The idea is to stay as close to the customer as possible to ensure, the PMF is achieved early on. Further, you should not be spending on marketing in the initial phases even if the funds are available. Only once the product/idea is established to be solving a real problem which can easily gain traction, you should think of marketing.

From the customers/target group perspective, as a founder you should know who your customer is and why do they fit to be your customer. Also, understand why someone aren't your customer. Your awareness or marketing strategy should be accordingly tuned to right and proper channels or outlets. For e.g. If you have developed a product for senior citizens, advertising in an IT park may not be a great idea considering the current demography of our country.

Next important element for a startup founder is the team that you need to build in. Initially considering the paucity of funds, you should be practical and choose your team very wisely. In case of a single founder, things are tougher than a two or more founders driven company especially if they are from different backgrounds and complement each other in different areas of business. However, having too many founders also pose a challenge at times; too many cooks spoil the broth. Once the founding team is final, next is creation of the A-team or a L1 team i.e. the senior leaders of the organization. In the initial phases of the company, usually, Product is the priority, hence companies hire head of Product, followed by head of Sales, and accordingly, Marketing, Finance and HR follow, depending on the need, stage of the company and the funds available. Ofcourse finding good team members is a challenge when you cannot afford expensive recruitment firms. The same can be done in various ways, including using your own network as well attending events, meetups, growth hacks etc.

All these boils down to the need to raise funds to develop the product, test it, market it, build teams etc. Hence, you should be aware of how much money is good from the business perspective that would be required initially to start off. Whether, you start with your own money or ask money from your friends or from angel investors, it is critical that you plan and know well the quantum of funds required. Practically, if the idea requires 8–9 months to ensure product market fit, and another 4–5 months to gain traction, reach some revenue or GMV, then you should raise money atleast to last 12–14 months. However, if you end up raising money for 8 months only, it doesn't mean you should not start, rather try to optimize and accelerate the processes to achieve the product market fit.

A CEO/founders' focal point should always be the team and the people across the journey of entrepreneurship. However, the focus may be different at different stages of the company. In early stages, product market fit is most crucial, thereafter once the PMF is achieved, and the company is in growth stage, the growth hack is important, once the growth is scaled, unit economics become essential to ensure to move towards profitability and then the fund-raise for the company is central.

With the above thoughts in mind, be informed, be educated, be positive and start with a leap of faith. Few nice one-liners, which may help you think positive:

- Become a jack of all trades.

- Have the "TEXAS attitude", when they win, they win big and celebrate, when they lose/go broke, they celebrate that too.

- Winning means being unafraid to lose.

- Be Unbalanced, it's okay to be shaky but keep moving forward.

- Do what you feel in your heart.

The king is always alone at the top, it's a tough and a lonely journey, but at the end its rewarding. Thus, all you need to do is ask yourself before taking the plunge, are you ready to take that challenge, run through the rough terrain and create your future in a beautiful way. Think and re-think and when your heart is not taking "NO" as an answer, just do it.

"Never Give up. Today is hard, TOMORROW will be worse, but the day after tomorrow will be SUNSHINE"

– Jack Ma, founder, Alibaba

Everyone thinks, entrepreneurship to be risky, however, a corporate job can actually be riskier, since you never know when you become a part of the lay-offs, needless to mention the Jet Airways shutdown and its most prominent outcome – thousands were left unemployed. The only thing certain in this life is uncertainty. Jobs are not safe because, businesses are not stable always. The best way to grow is to embrace change by learning to take risks as an entrepreneur and take charge of your own destiny.

Chapter 3

Organization Structure and Compliance

The moment you feel that you have piled up all the passion, commitment and dedication and now you can take that plunge to start up, the first dilemma that you as a founder find yourself landing into is, 'How to Start up?'

There are multiple questions to be answered before starting up. Broadly, the following need to be understood:

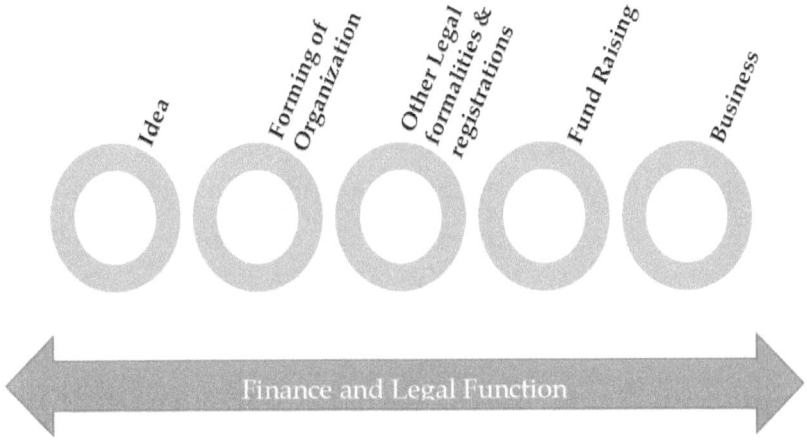

So, let's make the start-up idea simple to start-up!!! The first step to structure your idea is choosing the right form of legal Organization for your start-up. Often its commonly heard "I have started my Company"; "Did you register your Company?". Note that the word Company is used very colloquially in common parlance but it's important to note that, legally it is just one form of an Organization and there are various forms available. Hence, before one starts, one need to know the various forms of organization and evaluate what best fits the said business idea.

What are the legal formalities? How do I know the type of organization to start with? While there are pros and cons in each form, it is critical to evaluate and take a strategically wise decision.

The major forms of organizations are as follows:

a. Proprietorship Concern

Single owner called as Proprietor, simple and easy to form and can be started very quick.

b. Partnership Firm (Unlimited/LLP)

Two or more partners can form a partnership firm/LLP.

In a firm, a maximum of 100 partners are allowed, whereas in an LLP, there is no upper cap in number of partners.

c. Company (Private/Public/OPC)

A private company has minimum two members i.e. shareholders, a public company has minimum seven members, whereas an OPC (one Person Company) as the name suggests can be started by an Individual.

d. Trusts/Society/Non-Profit

Usually, there are three parties involved in formation of a trust. A contributor, Trustee and a beneficiary. A contributor/Sponsor/Settler creates the trust, Trustees manages them, and the beneficiary enjoys the benefit. These are used for philanthropy, social service, non-profit objective etc. A Society is formed for management of various social organisations like housing society, apartment maintenance, trade unions, trade associations etc. The Government also promotes these by extending various tax benefits, exemptions and subsidies.

The factors to be considered while evaluating the right form of Organization in India are Business, Taxation and Law/Compliances. Each of these are discussed in detail below:

a. Business

Business is the most crucial factor for the decision to start with a particular organisation structure. E.g. If the business demands a Private Limited Company, which would add value from a brand perspective and help generate traction, then one may go ahead with the same. One can always start with a proprietorship/partnership firm initially and once the business gets some traction, it can be converted into a private company. Optically, a company always sounds stronger, well established org when compared to other forms, enhancing the brand value and may be helpful in conversion of customers. Note, that the Investors put money only in private companies and not in firms or LLP. Once an investor shows interest, the business needs to be converted into a company.

b. Tax

The Taxation for each form of Organization is different as follows:

   i.   Proprietorship Concern – Taxed on slab basis of the proprietor

   ii. Partnership Firm (Unlimited) – 30% on the Net Income

iii.   LLP – 30% on the Net Income

iv.   Company (Private/Public/OPC) – The tax rate ranges from 15% to 30% subject to terms and conditions.

v.   Trusts/Society/Non-Profit – Depends on the nature – varies from tax exempt to conditioned taxability

Surcharge and Cess, as applicable, is in addition to the above taxes. The taxation rates mentioned above are as applicable for the year 2019/2020 in India. It is advisable to refer to latest changes and updates. *[Refer Annexure]*

There are a lot of structuring that can be planned in relation to the Org structure for companies that have global businesses and customers, employees scattered in different geographies. Eg. A Singapore holding Company with an Indian Subsidiary or vice versa. Overseas revenue being billed from Singapore and Indian customers from Indian entity, thereby benefitting from the lower taxes in Singapore. However, there are various factors to be evaluated before planning structures. Even business lines can be structured under different entities to optimise on the valuation, management as well taxation.

c. Law

i. Proprietorship Concern – Simple registration, no separate PAN required.

ii. Partnership Firm (Unlimited) – registration is not mandatory, though advisable, it is generally required by the bankers in case one opts for some bank loan.

iii. LLP – Governed by and registration under LLP law by the Ministry of Corporate affairs. The partners manage the firm.

iv. Company (Private/Public/OPC) – Governed by and registration under Company law by the Ministry of Corporate Affairs. Shareholders and Directors can be same person. Requires more compliance than an LLP. Trusts/Society/Non-Profit – Registration required under various laws like Society Act, Trust Act, Income tax approvals for exemption etc. These are suitable for Non-profit, NGO and philanthropy work.

d. Other factors

While forming an org., it is of great significance to think about the brand name which is a function of multiple legs like brand name, trademark, company name and the website.

Generally, brand name is chosen for the Product or the service being offered; the company name i.e. the legal entity name may work as a brand and the website domain/URL is equally important.

The brand name is an Intellectual property, that can be registered as a trademark, which gives a right to use the name and also a right to stop others from using it.

A brand name can be different from the Company name or the website URL (domain name). For example, a company may be named as *'Shamantic products Private Limited'*, whereas the product/brand name may be *"Shamaya"* and the website name may be *'Ayurveda.com'*.

However, it is best and advantageous when all the above are same from the marketing and brand perspective.

While registering a company, the first step is to choose a name. It is mandatory to do a trademark search and ensure that the same name/word is not someone else's registered trademark. Further, there should not be any other company with a similar name. The same restriction is there for LLP, however, there are no such restrictions in case of proprietorship or partnership firms, but from a long term perspective, it is always advisable to do the trademark search and also see if the domain name as desired is available, even if one starts with a proprietorship or a partnership firm. Infact, the domain name can be blocked, and trademark can be applied for early, which is not very expensive.

Trademark application is an online process, once applied for, one is allowed to use the symbol **TM** along with their logo or wordmark, which means trademark application has been filed. It usually takes 6 months (unless objected) for approval of trademark. Once approved, it is considered to be a registered trademark and the symbol ® can be used.

Once the organization is formed based on various factors discussed above, there are hordes of registrations, compliance and practical processes that is required to be followed in India:

Commercial Law (Practical Aspects)

- **PAN/TAN** – To be applied for as per Income Tax Act, 1961

- **Trade License** – Applicable as per local Municipal Corporation in few businesses (e.g. Hair Salon etc.) especially, where the municipal public property is being used.

- **Shops & Establishment (S&E)** – Applicable as per state laws and mandatory in most of the states.

- **Professional Tax (P.Tax)** – There are two types of professional tax compliance – (i) ENROLMENT as an organization and (ii) REGISTRATION as an employer, if there are more than certain number of employees in the company. In case of registration, P.Tax is to be deducted from employees salary and paid to the government every month.

- **Bank Account** opening in the name of the company for business.

- **Provident Fund (PF)/Employee State Insurance (ESI)** registration under EPF Act, 1952/ESI Act, 1948, if there are more than certain number of employees (presently 20 employees).

- **Goods & Service Tax (GST)** registration under CGST, SGST, IGST Act – Applicable in case of supply of goods or service above a certain threshold of annual turnover [Presently INR 2 Million (20 Lacs) for services and INR 4 Million for goods].

- **Import Export Code (IEC)** – Under Indian Customs Act, 1962 and Director General Foreign Trade (DGFT). For import or export of goods, IEC is mandatory, but, the same is not mandatory for export or import of services, however, it is advisable to take the IEC even in case of services to avail various incentives (SEIS scheme) provided by the government for export of services.

- **FEMA/RBI regulation** – Foreign exchange management Act – Cross border transactions are governed by these laws. Also, various financial companies like Banks, NBFC, fintech companies – payment gateways, micro financing, wallets etc. are governed by RBI regulations.

- **SEBI Regulations** – Securities and Exchange Board of India.

The listed companies are governed by the SEBI.

- **Environmental Clearance/Pollution** – The Environment Protection Act, 1986. Certain companies which manufacture or deal in hazardous substances, polluting materials or harmful to the environment are required to obtain registration under the environment protection laws.

- **DPIIT Registration** – To avail various startup benefits under the scheme by Government of India, it is advisable to register under DPIIT.

- **Other Licenses** – There are various licenses or approvals required specific to certain industries like FSSAI for Food industry, Medical licenses etc.

Each of the above registrations are required to be understood and applied for. There are variations depending on which part of country you want to startup, the state and the city too. Few laws are same across India while others are not. Hence, it is advisable to consult an expert before acting on any of the above.

Interesting Fact

PAN (Permanent Account Number) is a unique ten-digit alpha numeric number:

A	A	A	P	S	1	1	1	1	Z
1	2	3	4	5	6	7	8	9	10

- First 3 characters – Alphabets from AAA to ZZZ

- Character 6th to 9th – Numbers from 0001 to 9999

- Last 10th Character – Alphabetic Check Digit The 4th and the 5th character add twist to the tale:

- Forth character – This represents the status of the PAN holder i.e. **"P"** means an individual, **"F"** stands for firm, **"C"** stands for company, **"H"** stands for HUF, **"A"** stands for AOP, **"T"** stands for trust etc.

- Fifth Character – is the first letter of the holders last name/ surname; e.g. If the Name of the person is Raju **S**harma, the fifth Character would be **S.** In case of a Company or firm, the character would be first letter of the Company/firm's name e.g. If the company's name is Floater Private Ltd., the fifth character would be **F.**

Go ahead! Pull out your PAN card and check if the above is true.

Interesting Fact

Often, people get confused between a private company, public company and a listed company. The difference between a private and a public company was discussed earlier. These are two types of companies; however, a listed company is not a type of company but a status of a company i.e. whether the company is listed in a stock exchange or not.

Further, a condition for listing is that, it must be a public company, as the name suggests. Private company needs to be converted into Public company before listing. Hence, a public company can either be listed or unlisted. A startup is mostly registered as a private company and if it goes public i.e. gets listed, it is converted into a public company and then listed.

Chapter 4

Fund Raise

For starting a new business or for growing any running business, funds/ capital is required. The funds can be raised in the form of capital or debt. Fund raising is an Art or Science? Indeed, it is both an Art and Science. The first and the foremost pertinent thing around funding is **THE STORY** of your journey, company and its vision. Depending on the stage that one is in, it will have drama, action, colour. So, what's your story? The same genre or with variation should move across the talk, presentations, deck, numbers, metrics etc. Let's understand fund raise step by step.

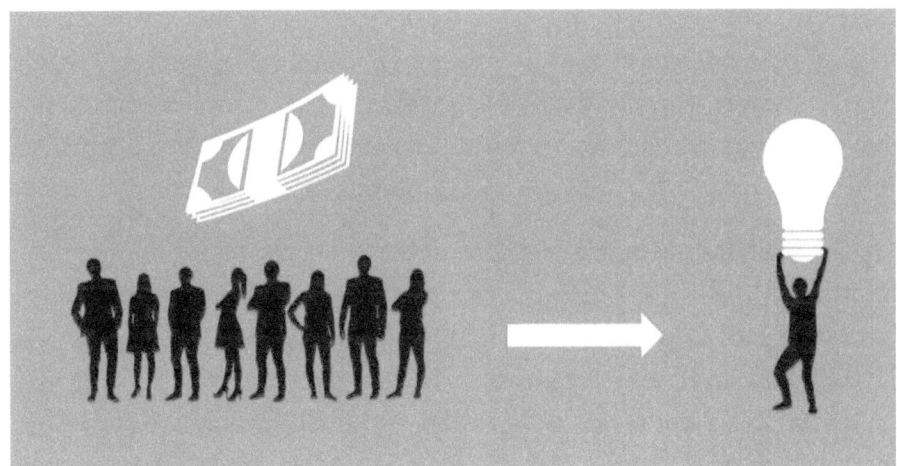

Types of Investors and its Stages

There are different stages of funding in a company. Traditionally, the only funds available were money borrowed and co-invested by friends and family or a bank loan. Banks do not provide loans without a mortgage in most of the cases. The development of the startup ecosystem in the last decade has gotten great interest from the Investor community and they are willing to take the risk of backing an idea of an entrepreneur, but what's in return? Of course making more money i.e. profits.

The New age (Startup) Investors can be broadly classified into the following categories:

a. Friends & Family (F&F)

b. Angel Investor

c. Venture Capitalist (VC)

d. Private Equity (PE)

e. Strategic Investor

Generally, VCs and PEs are considered as financial investor, whose ultimate motive is to make more money by investing in your business. F&F and Angel Investors are the people who support your idea at the very beginning to give you the initial kick start. Strategic Investors are Investor who come with a mindset of more than just money, they look for strategic tie-ups like technology exchange, business expansion, market reach etc., which in future may pave a way to Mergers & Acquisitions etc.

When an idea germinates in the mind of an entrepreneur and he starts on his own without taking money from the external Investors, it is called **Bootstrapped**. When he/she lacks capital, they look for someone to invest in their idea and form a company. The first ones to come forward may be family and friends, or one may find an initial financial investor, who are called Angel Investors and the initial round of funding is termed as **Seed Fund or an Angel round**. Well, are they really Angels in true spirit is something one must consider before accepting someone's money. The founders should not rush to grab the first money that they get access to. History says, there have been enough number of Angel Investors who made a fortune for themselves at the cost of business growth.

Once the company achieves some traction in terms of users and/or revenue, the interest of large investors kicks in, who have deeper pockets and capacity to write bigger cheques.

Venture Capitalists are Investors who back the company in early stages and have intention of making an exit in future rounds by selling their stakes to future Investors [Series A or Series B round of funding].

Private Equity are Investors who come in with an intention of owning a large chunk of the Company and generally want to see the company grow to the stage of Public offering/IPO i.e. getting the Company listed in a stock exchange [Series C, D, E and so forth]

Practically, the above terms are overlapping and should not be confused with. The terms fund, series, investors are interchangeably used.

Startup Funds Supply Chain

If you ask a student of commerce, a businessman or any rationale human being to state his business objective, the answer would most certainly be making profits. However, when it comes to Startup Investing, we very commonly hear that the Startups incur losses and burn cash but still Investor keep pouring in money to their kitty. The million-dollar question is "where is the damn profit then?"

To understand the above, let's take a step back and understand, who are the Investor(s) behind the Investor (VC/PE firms) who puts in money in startups. Basically, these are Retirement funds, family offices, super rich guys who do not know what to do with the money as they don't have more avenues for investment, they invest in the funds (VC/PE) [and are called LPs (Limited Partners) or GPs (General Partners) technically], who further invests in high risk growth opportunities to earn a good return. Usually, these funds in which they put their money has a fund lifespan of 8 to 12 years. Prior to committing the funds, GPs set fundraising targets and outline a strategy for the fund like industries, cheque sizes, regions etc.

Thereafter, the hunt starts for good startups and if a Fund invests in 20 great ideas (at least appears to be great apparently) and 19 of them fail, but, the one super star performer gives a return equivalent to 100x, which in effect may give an average return of 40% IRR (Return on Investment) on their portfolio, which sounds pretty attractive. Right ?

Here are some interesting insights on the Investor(s) mindset. The startup companies looking for funds may be desperate and some even consider the Investor(s) as God, if they found one. However, the truth is that, even they are humans working on payroll and trying to make good money to keep their Investors/LPs happy. Hence, there kicks in the famous FOMO (fear of missing out). For e.g. Investor A invests in UBER and it becomes a hype soon. The LPs of 'Investor B', would start bashing the fund managers for not being able to identify such opportunity. To cover that risk, B may start scouting for other similar companies say OLA, Taxi for Sure etc. and start investing in them. Hence, every company they Invest in, should not be perceived as a validation of a great idea always.

The Investors earn returns by exiting from a startup i.e. by selling their ownership in a company, commonly referred to as an Exit. At the time of Investment itself, the Investor and the founders/company discuss on exit options. The Exit options available are:

a. **Mergers & Acquisitions (M&A)** – One Company may be acquired by another. For eg. Redbus was acquired by South African internet and media giant Naspers for $140Mn and thereafter integrated with its Indian arm Ibibo group. The Investors of Redbus i.e. Inventus Capital partners and Helion Venture partners thus got an exit. Another example is Axis bank acquired Freecharge from Snapdeal.

b. **Initial Public Offering (IPO)** – If a company gets listed and shares are subscribed by the public, it is termed as IPO. e.g. In 2010, Make My Trip (MMT) got listed in Nasdaq (US stock exchange).

c. **Strategic Sale** – When few financial Investors sell their stake in the company to another financial Investor.

d. **Buyback** – Founders of a company may buy back the shares from the investors. A classic example of the same is OYO hotels, where the founder is contemplating a buyback of share from the Investors to increase his percentage ownership in the company.

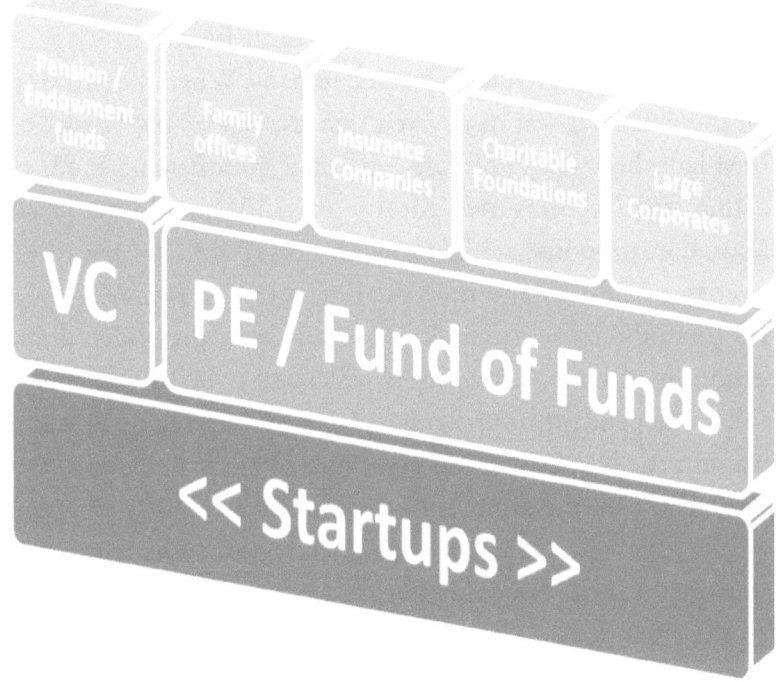

Startup Funds Supply Chain

Valuation

A bigger question, often unanswered by experts is, how does one value the company which is loss making and only burning cash. Theoretically, there are various methods of valuation namely, Discounted cashflow (DCF) method, Comparable Companies method, Multiples valuation (revenue multiple etc.), book value method etc.

However, we always wonder, how does the Investor value a company before Investing, when it is just an idea or is in initial stages of the company, with negligible revenues or profits. Let me get to the point straight and admit, there is no standard method of valuation and its mostly a vanity. Valuation would largely depend on the founder's power to negotiate and sell his idea. Few examples of valuing a company are:

Hypothetically, say a startup social media company named "Zunbro" (like Facebook), has 100 Million users in its platform, and the founders expect to earn $1 from each user in its foreseeable future (LTV), thus they demand a valuation of $100M for their company. When the Investors dug through the details, it was discovered that the out of 100M subscribers, only 70M have been active off late (say last 2 months) and the Investors argued that, their conservative guess is the LTV should be 50 cents a user. Thus, they proposed a valuation of $35M [70M x 50 cents]. Finally, they agree to a mid-way and the valuation agreed is $60M. Now, if one observes carefully, there are multiple variables in the above discussion like definition of users, active users, calculation of LTV per user etc. These all are dependent on the conviction and convincing power of the founders and the best estimation capability of both the parties. Further, taking a step ahead, the same can be compared to similar companies in the market. E.g. how many users does Facebook, WhatsApp, Tik-Tok have and what was the last valuation they raised money in. This process is called Benchmarking.

Company (Jul'19)	MAU (Billion)	Valuation ($Bn)	Value/User ($)
Facebook	2.41	570.00	236.51
Twitter	0.321	32.00	99.69
Netflix	0.152	147.00	967.11
Total	**2.883**	**749.00**	

To understand the valuation and the percentage ownership/dilution fundamentals, there are some financial terms that one needs to grasp:

Let us recall the terms from the 1st chapter:

1. Pre-Money Valuation

2. Post Money Valuation

3. Types of Shares – Equity (Common Shares) and Preference Shares

4. Dilution

To understand the math behind this, let us start with an example:

An Investor wants to fund a startup. There are two founders having equal ownership initially i.e. 50% each; and the Investor wants to invest INR 50 Million in the company. The founders and the Investor negotiate that for investing 50 Million, the pre-money valuation of the company would be 500 Million i.e. the Investor would get 10% stake in the company on a Pre-Money valuation basis.

Example: 1

Pre-Investment Cap Table		
Shareholder	Equity (No.)	%
Founder 1	100	50.0%
Founder 2	100	50.0%
Investor	0	0.0%
Total [A]	200	100.0%

Post-Investment Cap Table		
Shareholder	Shares (No.)	%
Founder 1	100	45.5%
Founder 2	100	45.5%
Investor	20	9.1%
Total	220	100%

Pre-Money Valuation – [B]	500
Add: Investment [C]	50
Post-Money Valuation	550

Price per share (B/A) [D]	2.5

No. of Shares the Investor gets (C/D)	20

In the given example, as the Pre-money valuation agreed is 500 Million and since the Investor agreed to invest 50 Million, the post money valuation increase to 550 Million. Price per share for this round of funding is calculated based on Pre-Money valuation (500) divided by No. of existing shares (200). The number of shares that the Investor gets is 20 (Investment amount divided by Price per share). It is interesting to note that the Post Investment, the ownership % that the Investor gets is not exactly 10%, but lesser than that, in this case, 9.1%.

One may note, due to issuance of shares to the Investor, the founders 1 & 2 diluted their stakes in the company by ~4.5% each i.e. in equal proportion. This is referred to as dilution in percentage ownership.

This is one way of calculating the ownership percentage, however, the conversation around valuation can be tricky at times, hence one must be careful on the wordings and be clear with the understanding and the expectations. For e.g. at times, in the first round of funding, an Investor may ask for a % ownership in the company, say 10% for Investing 50 Million in the company, which may essentially mean, the post-money valuation of the company is 500 Million (50 Mn/10%). In such cases the cap table would look as follows.

Example: 2

Pre-Investment Cap Table		
Shareholder	Equity (No.)	%
Founder 1	100	50.0%
Founder 2	100	50.0%
Investor	0	0.0%
Total [A]	200	100.0%

Post-Investment Cap Table		
Shareholder	Shares (No.)	%
Founder 1	100	45.0%
Founder 2	100	45.0%
Investor	22	10.0%
Total	222	100.0%

Pre-Money Valuation [B]	450
Add: Investment [C]	50
Post-Money Valuation	500

Price per share (B/A) [D]	2.25

No. of Shares the Investor gets (C/D)	22

Note: In the above example, the number of shares that the Investor gets is in decimal points, which is not practically possible (Shares cannot be issued in fractions), hence the same need to be adjusted. However, the same has not been adjusted and rounded-off.

One may note, due to issuance of shares to the Investor, the founders 1 & 2 diluted their stakes in the company by 5% each i.e. in equal proportion. This is referred to as dilution in percentage ownership.

Continuing the first example, let's assume, there is a second round of funding, and a new Investor shows interest and wants to Invest in the company. In this round, the founders and the new Investor 2 agree for a pre-money valuation of 1000 Million and the Investor 2 agrees to Invest 150 Million at this valuation. The existing Investor is also interested in participating in this round with a further follow-on Investment of 50 Million. The Cap table and the calculation is given below:

Example: 3

Pre-Investment Cap Table		
Shareholder	Shares (No.)	%
Founder 1	100	45.5%
Founder 2	100	45.5%
Investor 1	20	9.1%
New Investor	0	0.0%
Total [A]	220	100.0%

Post-Investment Cap Table		
Shareholder	Shares (No.)	%
Founder 1	100	37.9%
Founder 2	100	37.9%
Investor 1	31	11.7%
Investor 2	33	12.5%
Total	264	100.0%

Pre-Money Valuation [B]	1000
Add: Investment [C]	200
Post-Money Valuation	1200

Price per share (B/A) [D]	4.55

No. of Shares further issued (C/D)	44

Round Construct	Investment	No. of shares
Investor 1	50	11
Investor 2	150	33
Total	200	44

It is interesting to note that for Investor 1, despite investing the same amount of 50 Million in both the rounds of funding, the percentage ownership that he got were not the same. This is due to the change in valuation of the company.

The valuation is also a function of other factors like the Industry, funding environment, geography and what other startups in similar space are commanding. The comparison of the startup valuation with other companies is called Benchmarking.

A Sample Cap table is given in **Annexure A**

Valuation (Fair Value) by a Registered Valuer

As discussed above, it must be clear that the valuation for funding is more of a qualitative negotiation matter and may not necessarily be backed by real numbers. It is the way an Investor eyes the business and expects certain growth or market share of the company.

Whilst all these are practically true, legally there are various implications of the Valuation Report issued by a Professional, which is also mandatory in multiple cases as per different laws:

Valuation Report depicts the value per share i.e. the fair value per share as on a specified date, which is required for:

- Foreign Exchange Management Act (FEMA) – when overseas investors infuse money into Indian Companies, it falls under FDI (Foreign Direct Investment) guidelines which mandates that the Investment amount per share should not be less than its fair value.

- Income Tax Act (IT Act) – Section 50CA (Capital Gains) of Income Tax states that the sale value of shares of an unlisted company shall be deemed to be its fair value, if the actual sale value is less than the fair value..

- Companies Act – The Companies Act makes it mandatory to obtain a valuation report from a registered valuer for issue of shares under the law. This is required while filing various forms with the Registrar of Companies (ROC).

For the purpose of Income Tax act and FEMA, a valuation report from a SEBI registered Merchant Banker would suffice, however, for the Companies Act, a registered valuer under the Companies Act is required. Hence, it is important to plan the process well in advance.

An interesting factor while arranging a valuation report is that, generally, Investors prefer a lower (~15%-20%) calculated valuation than the actual transaction value. This is because of the Anti-dilution provisions. Just in case, the company issues shares at a lower valuation in the future, the adjustment through the conversion ratio is taken care of by a lower valuation certificate since then it does not violate the FEMA laws as discussed above.

Fund Raising Process

As discussed earlier, the primary ask of an early investor in the initial round or a seed funding stage is the founding team, their passion, capability, factored with the market size and the idea. Certain parameters along with these are adjudged by the potential investors and valuation is negotiated accordingly.

Apart from the above, as the round size increases and bigger fund houses show interest, the fund-raising process gets more formal and structured. The following depicts a quick snapshot of the process:

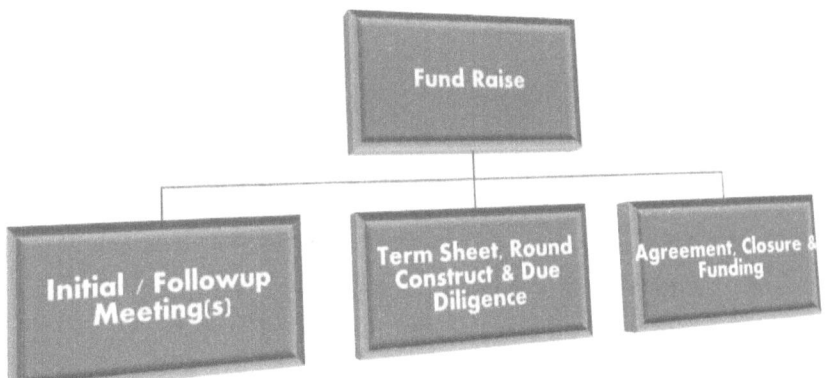

(a) Initial/Follow-up Meeting(s)

- Business Deck/Information Memorandum (IM)

- Business Model/Projections

- Prototype/Minimum Viable Product (MVP)

- Business Metrics

- Traction/Revenue

- End Use of funds/Deployment of funds

- Data Book/MIS

- Business understanding/Analysis

- Q&As/Negotiations

- Investment Bankers

As business starts to show traction *[Usually VC/PEs don't fund ideas unless it is backed by good traction]*, the founders/CFO can initiate setting up of initial meetings with the potential investors. First and foremost, a small deck/ teaser (2 or 3 Pager) may be prepared and shared with all the prospective investors comprising of key highlights of the business, like gross turnover, number of users, market size, nature of business etc. Once a prospect shows interest, a meeting is set up to understand the business in detail. These are followed up with detailed meetings and presentations. The investors ask for multiple data points for their analysis and feasibility study of the business, market size etc.

A summarized report (in MS Excel) in which a company tracks its key business metrics is called a Data Book or MIS. The data are presented in various forms like absolute numbers, percentages, ratios, trends etc. It presents the data from different angles like:

- Sales funnel – Traffic, signups, conversion, customers etc.;

- Revenue analysis – Product or service wise breakup, if the business has multiple offerings. Geography split, Demographic split etc.

- Impact metrics; market size etc.

- Financials – Profit & Loss account; Balance Sheet, Cash flow statement. This may also be drawn on the basis of various revenue models.

- Unit Economics/Operations – The business model viability from the operations angle and on a per unit basis. This is a very critical metric that every investor has a close eye on. The business viability is dependent on how the unit economics of the business is trending.

Detailed discussion on unit economics will be covered in the upcoming section.

On presentation of the data to the investors, they seek clarifications and responses to their queries to get an in-depth knowledge of the business.

It is critical to be clear on the purpose of funding and the usage of funds. Questions like these definitely come up during conversations, "Why do you want to raise $10Mn? What areas of business require investments? How do you plan to deploy thefunds? What is the delta or impact your investment plan will have?

To answer these questions, the management need to make a business plan (also called business model or financials model or projections) for the upcoming 3–5 years. Usually, the immediate one-year plan is expected to be water-tight, whereas the future years are more of an extrapolation of various numbers. For preparation of the business plan, the MS Excel come as a very handy tool and can work wonders if used in the right way. The Business plan consists of:

- **Revenue Assumptions** – Revenue streams; Basis of revenue i.e. No. of customers and Average Selling Price (ASP) from each customer. This can be further broken down into type and variety

- **Costs Assumptions**

  - Direct Cost – The Costs that are directly attributable to the product or service being sold/rendered

  - Indirect Costs – The costs that are not directly attributable to the product or service being sold/rendered

- **Sales Funnel** – The movement of the traffic to final conversion of the paid customer

- **Profit & Loss Statement** – Summarizing all revenue and costs and working out the estimated profit or loss number

- **Balance Sheet** – The position of assets and liabilities. This also depicts the plan to raise funds in the form of Debt or Equity

- **Cash flow Statement** – The status of cash in the business and future cash flow projections

- **Net Cash burn** – The Net cash outflow of the company

By and large, the supra is prepared on a monthly basis. i.e. if the projection is for 5 years, the data is prepared for 60 months forward. The business projections give a clear picture of the plan for deployment of funds and how the same would impact the business and the growth plan of the company.

As a founder, the intellectual outline of the key business metrics to be focussed on and a broad outline of the pitch deck to be presentedto the investors should be started well before time. Probably, even before you think of a fund-raise.

Often, founders are found baffled when it comes to deck preparation. The pitch deck is also called as Information memorandum (IM). There is no standard acceptable or formal pitch deck format that may be a winner. However, it is good to have the following information in the order:

- The Problem

- The solution i.e. the product/offering

- Market size

- Revenue Model/Projections

- Competitors

- Team

For any Institutional fund raise, as a founder, the pitch deck should always be in your mind even though it may be fuzzy initially, it can be well prepared eventually. There can be various business metrics, but it's important to identify the key headline, one or two metrics relevant to the business and workback towards the same with a clear timeline for oneself as well the team. e.g. GMV, Revenue or operational profitability. There is always a trade-of between different metrics, profit may be a trade-of with growth. Initially, growth and capturing the market share is more important than making the business profitable.

For the fundraise, the familiarity with the timeline is very imperative. You should always budget a good timeline say 2 months to 6 months from the initial conversation to the cash in bank. There are various steps and processes that one need to undergo for funding. To start with, selecting the right investment partner is crucial. Once the company grows, there may be various investors who may be interested and with experience, you get to know who are serious and who aren't. One easy hack is to identify companies in similar space and look for investors who have backed those companies. For example, if you are in a B2B business, it may be a complete waste of time to approach an investor who invests only in B2C businesses. These identifications will help whittle down the list and save a lot of time. Once you start meeting different Investors, just like any sales, be ready to be rejected and don't get disheartened. Also, ensure, every time an investor rejects or says "No", try to understand the reason for rejection, so that this experience can be used when you pitch in front of other investors.

It is good to practice enough for the pitch to the investors; it is akin to attending an interview and impressing the Investors in limited amount of time (Do look up 'Elevators Pitch'). It can be done through mock sessions, pitching in front of friends, experts, have some dry runs before the final marathon. The size of the market, the real solution to the problem at hand that you are trying to solve, the competitors etc. It is also good to have some background study done about the Investors which would be helpful in getting through that initial hurdle and keeping the conversation smooth.

Investment Bankers

Depending on the expertise and bandwidth within the finance team, one may plan to hire the experts in fund raising i.e. The Investment Bankers (IB) to run the fund raise process. The I.B.'s are a team of experienced players in the market who have the right investor connect and know how this game is played. They help companies in preparation of the data, projections, decks etc and do the hard part of selling the vision of the company, negotiations, valuations etc. Also, at times when there are large Investors on board, balancing their expectations and the round construct may not be an easy task, the Investment bankers comes in handy for having those uncomfortable conversations. Of course, the founder needs to sell his vision first or else no one can help. There is a famous idiom, which says *"If the founder can't sell his company, no one else can"*.

It is crucial to keep in mind that choosing the right and relevant Investment banker is important. There are various bankers in the field, but who is the right team for the task must be evaluated well. It is best to ask multiple bankers to take some limited data and present before the company why they should be hired for this mandate and what is their experience in the relevant industry and their Investor connects. Further, it is wise to take a feedback about the bankers from the Industry, their success rate and their credibility. There are many bankers, who undertake every project that comes by and are not able to close the round in all cases, their success ratio is very low, whereas there a few players who only take selective mandates and have 90%-100% success ratio.

Needless to mention that IB's come at a cost. Usually, they charge 1%-4% of the transaction value. Also, it is pertinent to mention that the % may be different depending on the round structure i.e. % fees will be lower, when it is raised from the Internals (Existing Investors), whereas it may be higher for new Investors onboarded.

(b) Term Sheet, Round Construct & Due Diligence

- Valuation

- Funding amount

- Macro terms

- Financial; Legal & Commercial DD

Based on the conversations, meetings, details and the data points shared with the Investors, if they find the business promising enough to invest, they issue a term sheet. A term sheet is a non-binding agreement between the prospective Investors and the Company, which generally includes the following:

- Investment Amount – E.g. $20Mn

- Type of Securities – E.g. CCPS

- Price/Valuation – E.g. $50Mn Pre-Money Valuation

- Terms of Preferred Shares – Dividends/Liquidation Preference Conversion/Antidilution/Other Rights

- Terms of Shareholder Agreements – Dividends/Liquidation Preference Conversion/Antidilution/Other Rights

- Disclaimer – The completion of the transactions contemplated by this memorandum will be subject to, among other things, satisfactory completion of financial and legal due diligence by the Investors, as well as the completion of final documents acceptable to the Investors.

There may be a few legally binding provisions too in a term sheet as follows:

- Confidentiality terms – The term sheet has this clause wherein the sensitive information about the company is protected from being shared by the prospective Investor(s) to third parties. It may have a validity too; say 2 years from the date of the agreement.

- "No-Shop Provision" or "No-Trade Provision" – This clause is to protect the prospective Investor(s). Through this provision, the company is prohibited from searching for any other financing with any third party for a specific period. It helps Investors in saving their time as well as their money by not getting involved in due diligence or negotiations with companies who are already talking to other potential investors.

A Company may receive multiple term sheets from different Investors depending on the conversation that goes with each one of them. Before the issuance of a term sheet, the Company and the Investors agree on the round valuation at which the Investor is ready to Invest.

Sample Equity term sheet(s) are given in **Annexure B**

Round Construct – When there are multiple Investors interested in participating in a round and it may include Investment from the existing

Investors (Internals), round construct becomes complex. At times, Investors have different expectations on percentage ownership in the company and the amount that they are willing to Invest. Some Investors may want a certain minimum percentage holding in the company or else may not be willing to put their bets on. In any round of Investment, the Investor who puts the maximum sum is called as a **Lead Investor** for the round. Generally, the major terms are negotiated with the lead Investor and others follow suit. However, the same may not be true always and negotiations may be done individually with all the Investors. Once, the valuation is set and the lead Investor is finalized, other Investor who may be willing to participate may also issue term sheets (or practically may not) and accordingly the final round construct is finalized.

Due Diligence (DD)

Post execution of the Term sheet with the Investors, a Due Diligence on the company is conducted by them. DD and Audit of books, sometimes used interchangeably, are two distinctive terminologies. Audit is done as it is mandatory under a relevant law, however, the DD is conducted by the Investor to ensure that the facts stated by the Company are correct and they know the company well before they Invest. Due Diligence is conducted by independent firms (may be a Big 4 accounting firm or otherwise; and legal firms). There are various types of due diligence-

- Financial Due Diligence (FDD) – This covers the financial transactions, assets and liabilities including the unit economics of the business. Finance and Tax DD are generally conducted by the same firm.

- Tax DD – This covers the taxation matters i.e. Direct (Income Tax) and Indirect (GST etc.). The aim is to ensure the company is in compliance with all the tax laws and the potential risks that may be involved in the company from taxation angle.

- Legal/Secretarial DD – Legal DD is conducted to ensure the company is in compliance with all the applicable laws like

Company law, labour law, has obtained all necessary licenses, etc. The Intellectual Property and ownerships are in place. One of the most critical aspect under legal DD is that the ownership of shares in the company are legally intact and there are no encumbrances or any risk on the ownership thereof.

- Commercial DD – Commercial due diligence is the process an Investor undertakes to gauge a company's commercial attractiveness. Unlike FDD, which focuses solely on the financial health of the company, this provides a full overview of the target's internal and external environment. Generally, this is undertaken by the Investor before signing of term sheet to evaluate the Industry and the target company.

Further depending on who gets the Due Diligence executed, there are two types of DD:

- Buy Side DD – If the firm (independent) conducting the due diligence is appointed by the Investor or a set of Investors, it is called a Buy Side DD. Every Investor may get the DD done independently which may be an expensive and time taking affair. Practically, all the Investors agree and appoint acommon firm and the scope is finalized and approved by all. The report of a Buy side DD is shared directly with the Investors confidentially.

- Vendor DD (VDD) or Sell Side DD – When the firm is appointed by the Company themselves, it is called a VDD. The biggest advantage of VDD is that it speeds up the process and saves costs. The VDD may be started well before getting the term sheet itself. Sometimes, the Investors accept the VDD report and may ask only for a top up for the areas that they may want to cover additionally. However, in case of VDD, since the appointment is done by the Company, they get to see the report and a chance to rectify the major lags.

In the DD report, the DD team classifies the observations into high risk, medium risk and low risk. Once the Investor gets the DD report(s), they hold discussions with the DD team as well the company on the major red flags. On reaching a consensus on the actionable, the Conditions Precedent (CP) and Conditions Subsequent (CS) are determined. Depending on the DD report and the findings, the Investors take a final call either to go-ahead with the Investment or may plan to drop the plan to invest, if there are some serious wrong doings in the company. At times, the valuation agreed in the term sheet too can be lowered, if the Investor is not convinced with the numbers presented earlier.

(c) Agreement, Closure and Funding

- Agreements – Definitive: SHA, SSA; Other agreements: Founders agreement; ESOPs

- Negotiation – Drag Along; Tag Along; Anti-Dilution; Board Seats; Pre-emptive; ROFO; ROFR, CP, CS etc.

- Cap structure – The Capital structure has been discussed in detail earlier

- Wiring of Funds

Definitive Agreements
Shareholders Agreement (SHA)

An agreement among the shareholders on their representations, warranties, rights and obligations. Some of the clauses, critical rights and which are negotiable in the SHA are:

a. Board Seat – The number of board seats that each of the Investor and the promoters may have. This is important since each board seat may have one vote and decides the fate of important decisions.

b. Board Observer – Small Investors generally have right to appoint board observers, who cannot vote but can attend the board meeting, but do not have any say in the meetings.

c. Voting Rights – The standard rule is 'one share-one vote' i.e. every shareholder (be it Equity shareholder or Preference Shareholder) gets one vote per share held. However, promoters or founders who are instrumental in starting a company often lose control of the firm when they dilute their stakes to raise multiple rounds of funding. Hence, Differential Voting Rights (DVR), which does not follow the standard rule and enables the promoters to retain control over the company, by allowing shares with superior voting rights (the promoter shares may have more than 1 vote per share). Thus, despite having less ownership in the company, they can have more control over the company affairs. The other way is, by issuance of fractional voting rights to non-promoters E.g. Investors/public shareholder(s) having fractional voting rights in case of a listed company.

d. Right of First Offer (ROFO) – In very simple terms, If a shareholder (e.g. Investor A) wants to sell his shares, the first offer should be made to the ROFO holder (E.g. Promoter), only if the ROFO holder does not exercise its right, A can sell the shares to any third party.

e. ROFR (Right of First refusal) –If a shareholder (e.g. Angel Investor C) gets an offer from a third party to sell his shares, the ROFR holder (e.g. Investor D), has the right to refuse such transaction and himself buy the shares at the same terms within the specified period.

f. Anti-Dilution Right – The shareholders especially Investors have a right to protect from equity dilution resulting from subsequent issues of shares at a lower price than the Investor originally paid. E.g. If the company issues further new shares to new shareholders at a lower/same price, the existing shareholders have the right *to change the conversion ratio in their favour/buy more shares in proportion to their holding,* such that their percentage stake in the company remains the same. Anti-dilution provisions are also known as pre-emptive rights, subscription privileges, or subscription rights. There are two types of Anti-Dilution – Full Ratchet and Weighted Average (Broad Based). Full Ratchet is not very common and is harsh on the founders. Weighted Average is common and widely accepted.

In some areas, Anti-Dilution and Pre-emptive rights are segregated like, Anti-dilution provisions are only used for a down round i.e. issuance of equity at a lower value however, pre-emptive rights give the right to further subscribe to the existing shareholders.

g. Tag Along Right – If a large Investor is selling its shares to a third party, small shareholders may have a tag along right i.e. force the large shareholder to ensure their stake is also sold along with them.

h. Drag along right – If a large Investor is selling its shares to a third party, it may have a drag along right i.e. to forcefully drag and ask the small shareholders to sell their stake along with them.

i. Transfer restrictions – The shares may have certain restrictions on transfer. E.g. Promoter may not be allowed to sell for certain number of years; Investors may not have right to transfer beyond a certain percentage without permissionfrom founders; Investors may not be allowed to transfer shares to competitors etc.

j. Liquidation Preference (Liq. Pref.) – Investors generally have preference over the founders/Angels in case of liquidation of the company. Many a times, the Liq. Pref. is multiple times of their investment. E.g. If the Liq. Pref. is 2x, it means, the Investor first gets twice the amount invested by them and thereafter the balance cash left is distributed in proportion to all the shareholders.

k. Exit Rights – The Investors generally have exit rights within a certain period (say 5 years) by way of an IPO, strategic sale or otherwise.

Interesting Fact

In the past, companies like Tata Motors, Pantaloon Retails and Jain Irrigation issued DVRs having fractional voting rights of $1/10^{th}$ of the Ordinary shares to public Investors. However, these shares offered higher dividend in lieu of voting rights being taken away.

Countries like USA, Canada, Singapore and Hongkong allow DVRs with strong monitoring and disclosure requirements.

Facebook issued two classes of shares – Class A shares carrying one voting right (listed through the IPO and held by public shareholders) and Class B shares carrying 10 votes each (not listed, held by Mark Zuckerberg and affiliates).

Share Subscription Agreement (SSA)

An agreement between the Company, Founders and the new incoming Investors on the terms of Investment, shareholding, representations, warranties, rights and obligations.

a. Conditions Precedent (CP) – These are conditions to be fulfilled by the company before the closure of the round.

b. Conditions Subsequent (CS) –These are conditions to be fulfilled within an agreed period (say 45/60 days) of the closure of the round.

c. Representation & Warranties – The Company and its directors provide many representations and warranties to the incoming Investors on the facts that has been stated in the agreement. For e.g. All the tax compliance is up to date.

d. Disclosure Letter – This is a disclaimer memo by the company on certain facts, which are not in sync with the Representations. In other words, these are exceptions, which the company is voluntarily disclosing and does not give an assurance that the same has been complied with. For E.g. Out of all tax compliance, the company discloses that the GST return for the month of May has not been filed. Now depending on the Investor's expectation, this may become a CP or a CS for the funding round.

e. Covenants – Various covenants are agreed upon by the company and the founders such as use of the subscription amount as per the approved business plan, confidentiality, publicity, FDI compliance etc.

f. Capitalization table – Pre and Post closing capitalization (cap) table forms part of the SSA.

One important factor in case of an overseas investor is the exchange rate for conversion of funds from foreign currency to Indian Currency (INR). There are two ways in which this is dealt with; if the term sheet and the amount in SSA is agreed in foreigncurrency (say USD), then the company's banker (Authorized Dealer (AD) as per RBI guidelines) will receive funds in USD. These funds will then be converted by the AD banker and credited to the company's capital/current account. In this case, the company needs to negotiate with the bank on the exchange rate to be used for conversion on the date of funds transfer. The Company takes the exchange risk in this scenario.

In the other case, the exchange rate is agreed upon between the Company and the Investor. The SSA has the Investment amount in INR. Hence, it's the investor's responsibility to ensure that the exact amount INR is credited to the Company's account.

Closure and Funding

On finalization and execution of the SHA and SSA, the company ensures and completes all the Conditions Precedent (CP) and gives a declaration to the Investor that all the CPs have been complied with. Thereafter, the company issues a subscription notice to the Investors. Post which the funds are wired/transferred to the company's bank account. Post closure, the company is required to fulfil the Conditions Subsequent (CS) and comply with various FEMA and FDI laws. The AD banker's involvement is critical here to ensure proper FIRC and KYC documents are received to comply with the filings in the RBI/FEMA portal e.g. FIRMS portal.

A sample CP completion letter and Subscription Notice is given in **Annexure C**

Primary Issue of Shares and Secondary Sale

Primary issue of shares means issue of new equity shares by the company i.e. legally creating new stocks and issuing them to subscribers, whereas secondary sale means sale of shares from one shareholder to another shareholder, the company does not issue any new shares in case of a secondary sale, it is just a transfer of ownership from one hand to another.

In case of a primary issue, the total outstanding shares of the company increases and has an effect on ownership percentages of all the shareholders of the company and thus is governed by various provisions in the SHA like Anti-dilution, pre-emptive,ROFO, ROFR etc. Every time a company raise more money from new/existing shareholders, a new SSA is entered into with the subscribing investors and an amended and restated SHA is executed among all the shareholders including the new ones.

In case of a secondary sale, an existing shareholder may sell his/her shares to a person, who is not a shareholder in the company already, in such a case, the new shareholder has to commit that he/she would comply with all the provision of the existing SHA. No new SHA is re-executed for the new shareholder, instead the same is achieved by execution of Deed of Adherence (DOA) between the new shareholder and the company. In the DOA, the new incoming shareholder promises to adhere to the terms and conditions of the SHA as was agreed by the selling shareholder. A Deed of Adherence is a document by which a person/entity becomes a party to an existing Shareholders' Agreement

A sample Deed of Adherence is given in **Annexure D**

Apart from the above, there are few other major agreements/plans that one must know and are critical:

Memorandum of Association (MoA) and Articles of Association (AoA)

When a new Company is formed, there are two major documents Memorandum of Association (MoA) and Articles of Association (AoA). MoA is the Charter of the Company i.e. the foundation of the company which defines the constitution and scope of powers of the company. MoA cannot override the Company law. Whereas AoA are the byelaws of the company i.e. set of rules and regulation to manage the internal affairs of the company. The AoA cannot override the MoA. It may be noted from the fund-raising perspective that, AoA is almost a replica of the SHA, which essentially means, all the rights and obligations agreed in a SHA is copied into the AoA to give the agreed covenants more legal colour and authority.

Founders Agreement

An agreement among two or more founders along with the company specifying their authorities and responsibilities such asshare of ownership, guaranteed obligations of different founders as well defining their roles, responsibilities, targets, expectations, remunerations, equity vesting schedule etc.

Initially, when a company is started by friends and like-minded founders, everything looks promising & rosy as one is positive & feels that nothing can go wrong between them. However, when things get gloomy and the going gets tough in business, discussions are not very smooth and may end up as a disagreement among the founders, especially on the responsibilities and faults. Hence, it is advisable and professional to have a founders' agreement in place to avoid any kind of situation that may hinder the relationship among the business owners.

ESOP Plan

Employee Stock Options are options given to employees to own shares/ownership in the company. This helps in keeping the employees interested, motivated and stick to the company they work with. Often, in early stage companies and startups, ESOPs are a vital tool to retain employees and compensate them in a form other than cash. The idea is to create interest by having their skin in the game.

An Employee Stock Option plan is approved by the shareholders and the Board on the terms of the options to be offered to employees like vesting period, vesting conditions (time or performance or both), exercise price etc. The shares issued upon exercise of options is Equity or Common shares. The plan is subject to various laws like Companies Act, Income Tax Act etc. Generally, ESOPs are issued to employees. There are conditions to be met under the law, in case the ESOPs are to be issued to promoters or directors of the company. The ESOP taxation is tricky and has been discussed in the Appendix.

Insurance Policies

You may wonder, why is Insurance Policy being discussed here. Considering the risk involved in everything we undertake; Insurance sector has widened its reach to new interesting risk coverages in the market today. Even, the Investors insist on taking some of these coverages to safeguard their interest. It is important to know brieflyabout them:

Apart from varied insurances such as health, life, accidental, asset, fire etc. that the organisations take for their business and employees, there are a few third-party liability covers which are critical:

a.   Director & Officers (D&O) Policy – Directors and Officers liability Insurance (often called "D&O") is liability insurance payable to the directors and officers of a company, or to the organization(s) itself, as indemnification (reimbursement) for losses or advancement of defence costs in the event an insured suffers such a loss as a result of a legal action brought for alleged wrongful acts in their capacity as directors and officers. Such coverage can extend to defence costs arising out of criminal and regulatory investigations/trials as well; in fact, often civil and criminal actions are brought against directors/officers simultaneously. Intentional illegal acts, however, are typically not covered under D&O policies. [Source: Wikipedia].

This is important from the fact that, if a third party sues the company and make the directors and officers party to the claim, this policy safeguards the individual promoters, directors and Investor directors.

b.   Commercial & General Liability (CGL) – This Insurance cover the risks on third party bodily injury or property damage on the business premises or due to the business operations, personal and advertising injury, and medical payments.

c. Professional Indemnity (PI) – Professional Liability Insurance (PLI), also called Professional Indemnity Insurance (PII) but more commonly known as Errors & Omissions (E&O) in the US, is a form of liability insurance which helps protect professional advice – and service-providing individuals and companies from bearing the full cost of defending against a negligence claim made by a client, and damages awarded in such a civil lawsuit. [Source: Wikipedia]

d. Cyber Insurance – Cyber-insurance is an insurance product used to protect businesses and individual users fromInternet-based risks, and more generally from risks relating to information technology infrastructure and activities. [Source: Wikipedia]

Unit Economics and Cash Flow

Unit Economics plays an important role from the business finance/FP&A angle. Even the Investors look for and track the unit economics very closely. Let's understand why the unit economics or operative metric is so vital.

Few terms that we shall use here are Revenue, Direct Costs, Indirect Costs, Fixed Costs, Variable Costs, CAC, Gross Margin, Contribution Margin. To make a clear depiction of these terms, please follow the table below:

Particulars	Amount
Revenue	100
Direct Costs	-60
Gross Margin	40
GM%	40%
Indirect Costs	-20
EBIDTA	20
EBIDTA%	20%

Table 1

Particulars	Amount
Revenue	100
Variable Costs	-50
Contribution Margin	50
CM%	50%
Fixed Costs	-30
EBIDTA	20
EBIDTA%	20%

Table 2

The above Profit and Loss statement which has equal Revenue, Total Cost and EBITDA has been drawn in two different methods which brings out the distinction. In the first P/L (Table 1), direct cost (Costs directly attributable to Revenue) has been reduced to arrive at the Gross Margin, then the indirect cost (Costs not directly attributable to Revenue) is reduced to arrive at the Profit. This is a standard way in which a PL is drawn for reporting/accounting purposes.

However, from an analytical angle, Table 2 is different, the variable costs (Costs that vary with every unit of revenue, say the product sold) are reduced from revenue to arrive at the Contribution margin. The expression contribution itself suggests that per unit of product sold contributes × amount to the business. Thereafter all the fixed costs are reduced to arrive at profits. It is Interesting to note that, the direct costs of 60 (Table 1) consists of both fixed (10) and variable (50) nature of costs (Table 2).

The contribution margin helps us understand, whether the business is operationally profitable or not i.e. Whether the contribution margin is positive. Now, let's take an example with a detailed PL:

Particulars	Amount	Units Sold	Amount Per Unit
Revenue	1,00,00,000	10,000	1,000
Variable Costs	-50,00,000	10,000	-500
Contribution Margin	50,00,000	10,000	500
CM%	50%		50%
Fixed Costs	-80,00,000		
EBIDTA	-30,00,000		
EBIDTA%	-30%		

The above PL suggests that the company is making a loss of 30 lacs (3Mn) in the period, but the CM is positive to the tune of 50 Lacs (5Mn), which means operationally the business is doing great, but the fixed costs are very high. On a per unit basis, the company is making a profit of Rs. 500 per unit, which essentially means, if the company sells 16,000 units, the company will be breakeven, and every unit sold above 16k, will give a net profit of Rs. 500.

$$\text{Units to be sold (for breakeven)} = \text{Fixed Costs/CM per unit}$$
$$= 80 \text{ Lacs}/500 = 16,000$$

The above makes it amply clear, that if the company can sustain and increase the volume from current 10,000 units to 16,000 + units, it is a great business to be in. To a layman, observing the above, one may feel, business is bad, however, an Investor looks at the business from an unit economic business angle to see if the business can scale, increase the volume to capture the market share and really make money in the future. Precisely the reason most of the startups are burning cash and are in deep red, while they create the market for themselves by acquiring customers.

This brings us to another important discussion on the unit economics:

Particulars	Amount Per Unit		
Revenue	100		
Variable Costs	-50	Revenue/CM1:	
Contribution Margin 1	50	100/50 = 2	RevenueCAC:
CM%	50%		100/60 = 1.7
CAC	-60		
Contribution Margin 2	-10		
CM%	-10%		
Fixed Costs (Absolute Value)	-80,00,000		
EBIDTA	xxx		
EBIDTA %	xxx		

[Customer Acquisition Costs (CAC) comprises of the sales and marketing costs incurred to acquire the customer. Generally, it does not include the brand building costs].

In the above table, the CM has been calculated at two levels i.e. CM1 and CM2. CM1 is positive Rs. 50 per unit. However, after reducing the Customer Acquisition Cost (CAC), the CM2 is negative, which means, to earn Rs. 50 from a customer, the company is spending Rs. 60 to acquire the customer, which apparently looks to be a not-so-good strategy (This depicts why the customers get so much of cashbacks!).

From the above PL, to breakeven at the CM2 level, the ideal breakeven ratio of *Revenue/CAC* will be equivalent to *'Revenue/CM1 i.e. 100/50 = 2'*, which essentially means, if the ratio of *Revenue/CAC* is 2, there is no profit no loss and we are breakeven, since if we spend CAC of 50, the CM2 becomes zero. In the above example, the *Revenue/CAC* ratio is 100/60 = 1.7, which means we are not at breakeven and incurring losses. Let's dig a leveldeeper, imagine, if the same customer comes back to our platform and purchases a second product, our CAC per customer does not change, since the customer is a repeat customer, but gives us the CM1 of 50 × 2 = 100, against which we spend a CAC of 60 only, thus making a CM2 margin of 40. Suddenly the *Revenue/CAC* ratio becomes 200/60 = 3.33, which is good.

This repeat customer's revenue/margins (through retention of customers), is called Life Time Value (LTV) of the customer, which typically means, if the customer stays in our platform and purchases our product, how much money will the company make till the time it is able to sell the products again and again without incurring additional marketing spends on him/her.

Thus LTV/CAC gives the clear picture of the business performance and is a very common metric used to gauge businesses' operational health by the Investors.

It is important to understand that the LTV of a Customer can be viewed in two different ways:

1. Revenue/Sales from the Customer × No. of repeat purchases = Total Revenue that we expect to generate from a customer

2. Contribution Margin (CM) from the customer × No. of repeat purchases = Total Margins that we expect to generate from a customer.

Hence, while communicating, it is good to be clear on the correct reference to either LTV (Margins) or LTV (Revenue), since it impacts the equation and ratio significantly.

Another critical metric that is tracked is called Churn i.e. the customers dropping out from the system. The companies, which follow the SaaS (Software as a Service) model or a Subscription model of revenue, the LTV/CAC and churn are the most important metric to be tracked even from the internal business perspective.

The various costs discussed above may sometimes have an element of subjectivity; for instance, a particular cost item which is an indirect cost but also 100% variable, there may be questions around would it form part of the contribution margin E.g. payment gateway charges for collection of revenue. There can be various similar dilemmas. The answer to the same would depend on theindustry, nature of business model and the company. There may also be a cost item which may be partially variable and partially fixed in nature, best is to bifurcate the same to get the correct picture. Now, one can make sense that once we understand the unit economics well, only then a strong grip on the business is possible.

It is advisable for every entrepreneur to keep a close tab on the unit economics of business from the very beginning since this works like a nerve of the company. More often than not, companies in their desire to expand and gain the market share, forget the operational metrics, which costs them a lot in later stages.

From an Investor pitch perspective, there are various hacks that can be/are being used by entrepreneurs worldwide. For instance, if the company operates in multiple cities, the company can prepare city wise P/L and showcase profitability in one city and go to the investors and claim that if one city can be profitable, it can be easily replicated to other cities. This may be true considering it's the same management running the business but could not be done presently due to want of funds. There are other ways too to showcase positive unit economics by considering pre-variable cost profitability, pre-marketing profitability since every business is different and Investor do respect your thoughts if the same is aligned to the model.

Cash Flow

In finance, they say, **REVENUE IS VANITY; MARGINS ARE SANITY; and CASH FLOW REALITY**

We discussed on the revenue and the margins in detail, cash flow is a super critical metric that the investors are concerned about and also the promoter should be aware of. The above phrase makes it clear that revenue is just a vanity metric unless supported by the cashflows.

Once basic question is why is cashflow important? Imagine a company which gets a lot of orders from its customers and sells its product at very high margins, however, it sells the products on credit of 45 days. The customers do not pay within the credit period, to add to the woes 40% of the time they default on payment which the company has to write-off in their books. If one glances at the P/L of such a concern, its revenue may look great, the marginsand the unit economics may look promising. The company however is unable to collect its receivables and thus fails to generate proper cashflows. Reality is that the revenue and the margins reported are not correct in true sense. Business may appear favourable prima facie from the outside, but the health of the business may be in a bad shape if collections are not tracked properly. Irregular monitoring or tracking of the cashflows shall adversely impact other expenses and outflows of the company. Further the entire budgeting and planning may go haywire. Hence, as a part of the MIS, databook as well other reports, Cashflow makes such an ingredient to the P/L as salt is to food.

Cohorts

A cohort is a group of data of common characteristics. Cohort data analysis is very helpful in analysis and can give astonishing results. Even the investors love the data presented in cohorts as it gives a great insight of the data facilitating in decision making.

Let us understand the same through an example, say a company (subscription model) acquired 360 customers in a quarter Apr-Jun. In July, 220 customers continue to avail the service, the company has a retention of ~61%. However, once we do the cohort analysis i.e. group the customers based on the month of acquisition, the following is revealed.

No. of customers		Acquisition Months		
		Apr	May	Jun
Retention Months	Apr	100		
	May	90	110	
	Jun	60	50	150
	Jul	60	40	120
	% Retention (Jul)	60%	36%	80%

The above table shows the customers, who joined in April and June had 60% and 80% retention respectively. However, the retention of customers joining in May dropped significantly to 36%. Further deep diving into May data revealed that due to some technical glitch, there were huge drop out in the month of June, which is also evident for April cohort customers dropping from 90 to 60 in June. Thus, these kinds of analysis are really helpful.

Debt Vs Equity

To run a business, a company needs capital, which can be in the form of Debt or Equity. We discussed on the Equity fund raise in detail form a startup perspective. However, Debt is also an important mode of raising funds. The Debt raise by a company is known as Leverage. The question is how much a company should be leveraged.

An important metric called Debt to Equity Ratio is calculated as follows:

Debt to Equity Ratio = Total Liabilities/Shareholder's Equity

A high debt to equity ratio indicates a business uses debt to finance its growth. Companies that invest large amounts of money in assets and operations (capital intensive companies) often have higher debt to equity ratios. For lenders and investors, a high ratio means a riskier investment because the business might not be able to earn enough money to repay its debts.

Theoretically, the ideal Debt: Equity (D/E) Ratio is in the range of 1 to 1.5, which means, if the Equity (owners' money) is 1 Crore, the company should not borrow more than 1.5 Crores. Further, if the Debt cost (interest) is 10% and the company can earn 15% from business, it means, the company is making extra 5% for its shareholder (owners of the company) since, the Debt lenders will get only the fixed return in form of interest, but the shareholders participate in earnings of the company, hence they take a larger risk. Thus, more the Debt, it's better for shareholders if they can make more return from the same. Hence, there is always a trade-off between Equity and Debt as to how much a company can raise in form of Equity and how much through Debt. With reference to Startups, say a company is raising a $50M round, at a valuation of $500M, it means all the existing shareholders will dilute their holding by 10%, whereas if the company can raise $10M in Debt and $40M in Equity at the same valuation, the dilution would only be

8%, that saves 2% dilution in percentage ownership of the company. Hence, it is important to leverage at times. There are further multiple reasons for leveraging the company, like it helps increase the runway for the company, it helps save taxes if thecompany is profitable since the interest on tax is allowed as business expenditure. When a company has surplus cash (extended runway), it is able to command a better valuation during negotiation as it has more time at its disposal to discuss and negotiate with multiple potential investors. It gives the company an upper hand and helps negotiate from a position of strength and not weakness.

Financial Instruments

There are various types of financial Instruments. The most commons ones are Equity Shares (Common Shares), Compulsorily Convertible Preference Shares (CCPS) and Non-Convertible Debentures (NCD).

- Equity Shares (Common) – The holders of Equity share are the owners of the company and have the dividend and voting rights. Promoters and employees mostly hold Equity shares.

- Preference shares – Preference shares gives the holders a preferential right over common share i.e. in case of liquidation (sale or closure of business), these holders have the first right to money/assets in the company i.e. in the distribution of assets/cash, preference shareholders get a preference over the common shareholders. This is called Liquidation Preference. The Investors mostly prefer Preference shares when they invest in a company and have various extra rights over the Equity shareholders. Even the Preference share have voting rights.

- Debentures – These are instruments against the loans taken by the company. The basic difference between a bank loan and Debenture is that, only banks and NBFC can lend as per the RBI guidelines, however, if the company wants to borrow from any other third party, there are various restrictions, hence companies issue debentures. The debenture holders are also protected by law and require appointment of Debenture Trustee who ensure the safety and rights of the Debenture holders.

Further, depending on the need and circumstances, there can be multiple classes of shares e.g. Class A Equity, Class B Equity, Series A CCPS, Series B CCPS, Series A Debentures. At times,differential rights (voting rights, dividend rights etc.) are created among the shareholders by forming multiple classes of shares or due to different face value of each share.

It is to be noted that the shareholders are owners of the company whereas the company is indebted to the lender/Debenture/bond holders. There are a variety of instruments that can be created and are allowed as per law. For instance, convertible Debentures, Non-convertible Preference shares etc. It is critical to determine the real essence of the instrument (substance over form), for e.g. In case of a convertible debenture, it is not a pure debt but a quasi-equity since it can be converted into equity and the holders can become a shareholder. This is important from understanding the nature of financing as well the accounting perspective as Accounting Standards (AS) or the International Financial Reporting Standard (IFRS) requires us to identify the true nature of the instrument and book the asset/liability accordingly.

In common parlance, when a company raises funds, it is said to be an equity raise, however, there can be various instruments technically.

Face Value & Premium:

Every issued share has two components associated with it, Face Value (also called Par value) and Premium. Say, a share has a face value (Nominal Price) of Rs. 10, it means every share issued would be of minimum Rs. 10/- fully paid up. Based on the agreed valuation (See Topic Valuation), if the price per share comes to Rs. 100, it means that the investor is paying a premium of Rs. 90 (100 – 10) per share to acquire those shares.

The implication of the above are manifold:

a. Authorized Share Capital

    Under the Companies Act, every company must pay fees to the ROC (Registrar of companies) for authorized capital along with stamp duty. The Authorized capital comprises of nominal value only. Hence, higher the face value, higher the fees/stamp duty cost.

b. Income from Other Sources (Angel tax) [Abolished in Budget 2024]

    The Income tax law states, amount paid over and above theface value i.e. premium which exceeds the fair value of the shares, is taxable in the hands of the company. However, there are exemptions for certain funds and companies on fulfilment of certain conditions.

c. Future use of Securities premium

    The Securities premium can be used for issue of bonus shares, for buy back of shares and other utilization(s) subject to conditions as per law.

Interesting fact:

Every country across the world does not have the concept of par value and the premium. For instance, Singapore in 2006 abolished the concept of par value and securities premium, there is just a share price at which the share are issued to the subscribers.

Venture Debt

These are loans provided by the lenders (either banks or non-bank lenders) to venture backed companies for working capital requirements, acquisitions, assets purchase etc. Practically, startup companies do not have access to traditional bank funding since they do not have assets to mortgage or any other security against which the banks may lend; they are also not profit making, which makes it very difficult for banks to lend. Thus, the venture debt business has seen a steep rise in number of players as well the funds being deployed in India recently.

Venture Debt companies generally lend to startups which are backed by equity investors and have sufficient cash in their kitty. This ensures that the business model looks viable (precisely the reason an VC/PE may have invested) and their money is safe (enough cash in bank). The major terms in a venture debt arrangement are listed below:

a. Coupon Rate – Interest rate payable monthly e.g. 15% p.a.

b. Processing Charges/Commitment fees – e.g. 1% flat on the Drawdown amount or on the full commitment amount.

c. Redemption Premium – percentage of the loan amount to be paid along with the last instalment.

d. Right to Subscribe (RTS)/Warrants – Right to subscribe to xnumber of shares of the company at an agreed valuation in the next 6–7 years of time. E.g. 10% flat worth of the loan amount lent to the company. The Investors generally exercise this right only in case the value of the company increases in the future rounds or at the time of exit. Hence, they do not have any risk since they did not invest any money and hold only the right and not an obligation. If this works out well in their favour, their IRR from the portfolio company looks very good.

e. Right to Invest (RTI) – Typically, Debt Investors ask for a right to invest in future rounds of funding at par terms with other investors in case they wish to. They may or may not exercise this right.

f. Drawdown Tranches – If the loan is taken in multiple tranches and not in one shot (Bullet), it is called drawdown in tranches.

g. Moratorium Period – The period in which principal repayment is not done, say 6 months. E.g. The principal repayment shall start only after 6 months of the first drawdown. At times, even interest repayment may enjoy the moratorium, if agreed upon.

h. Prepayment charges – The charges to be paid in case the company wants to prepay the loan before the scheduled pay-out dates. Also called as Early closure charges.

i. Penal Interest – Extra interest in case of default or delay in repayments.

Typically, a Venture Debt Investor aims to make a return of 20%-23% IRR on their portfolio.

Recently, new venture debt companies have started offering debts even without warrants but demand a redemption premium i.e. additional amounts along with the last instalment payment (say 10% of the loan amount), this gives them an assured return in the range of 20%-23%, which is a significantly good return compared to various other class of assets. Considering the developments in this space, few traditional banks have setup startup offices to offer venture debt in similar fashion.

Interest and processing fees are common even for traditional lending banks, however, in case of venture debt, they even expect

RTS and RTI for taking an additional risk in a loss-making company. Depending on the legal structure (NBFC/Bank/AIF) of the debt investor, RTS or warrants are issued. Further, a simple loan can be given by an NBFC (Non-Banking Financial Company) whereas if the Investor is not an NBFC, Non-Convertible Debenture is issued.

Few sample venture debt term sheet(s) are given in **Annexure E**

Chapter 5

Finance Function

One thing that haunts any CEO or a business owner is the thought of complying with the innumerable regulations in India and simultaneously managing bureaucratic officers. Finance, not being a direct revenue-generating function, is often neglected by the top management initially. However, subsequently it ends up squeezing major chunk out of their pockets, in terms of cost of hiring good finance personnel, clearing the past nuisance created due to lack of proper financial planning, penalties for non-compliances, and so forth.

They fail to decipher that finance being a core business-enabling function forms an indispensable part of every organisation's growth story. Finance facilitates cost cutting, charting out better investment avenues, understanding strategic roadmaps and structuring deals.

Ideally, once the Series A funding round is closed, the first priority of a CEO/founder should be to get on board a senior qualified finance professional who can steer the wheel of the ship in the right direction along with the management. Many startups that fail to recruit an able finance person end up paying large sums to consultants as they do not possess adequate finance knowledge internally. After Series A, and in cases when the Series A fund raise is not very large, startups can opt for Virtual CFO services or outsourced finance services provided by independent finance professionals.

The entire finance function can be broadly categorised into three parts – finance controllership, investor relations & business finance; and fund raising & treasury. Here are some of the key areas that require ones' attention from the very inception:

Study, Compliance and Process Management

a. **Laws of various geographies in which the company operates or is planning to operate.**

The laws prevalent in various countries are diverse and need to be complied with. For example, social security law may not be that strict in India, whereas it is a nightmare in the US or other western countries when not complied with. On the other hand, the transfer pricing regulations may be a cakewalk in Tokyo when compared with the draconian annual compliance rules in India. Further, even within the country, the laws vary from state to state and more often than not, local municipality regulations are equally important to comply with.

b. **MIS Reporting and Presentation**

The investors who have put in money in your company deserve to be periodically updated about the whereabouts of the company and the target their portfolio is heading to. A good finance professional knows the critical metrics required to be presented to the investors, hand in hand helping the management to keep a close tab on the control points. Thus, the MIS preparation, reporting and board presentations are strict and important artefacts that cannot be shunned.

c. **System automation, CRM etc.**

The company should start automating its process from the initial stages and having the effective CRMs (SAP, Salesforce etc.), accounting software (Tally ERP, SAP B1, QuickBooks etc.) in place. It is always easy to capture and decode the data when the organisation is in the developing phase and further collate it for the next level of growth, whether you want to impress the incumbent investors or pass the due diligence test smoothly.

Financial Planning & Control

Listed below are the key areas which any startup should eye for healthy growth and strong internal control:

a. **Fund management & Investments** – Positive cash flows and low working capital is something every CFO strives to achieve. However, to operate at zero/negative working capital may be a distant dream. Also, the cash should not be kept idle and one must strive to invest and earn the minimum opportunity cost relevant to the funds, keeping in mind its safety and recoverability.

   i. **Optimum cash management**

   It is important that cash inflows and outflows are managed well. The same can be achieved by preparing budgets, estimating revenue collections and the spends of the company. An ideal way is to have an Annual Operating plan for the company broken down into quarterly and monthly budgets and further broken down into functionary budgets. Every dollar outflow should ultimately add value to the company.

   ii. **Treasury Management**

   Based on the budgetary plans discussed above, a company will have idle cash sitting in their banks, which needs to be invested optimally to generate good returns without risking the principal i.e. capital. Further, when a startup raises a large equity round and is sitting on a large pile of cash, it is pertinent to explore the best options and invest.

There are various options one can invest the idle funds into. The Investment objective in case of a startup should be as follows:

- Safety – Investment avenues identified must be such that at no point in time, undue risk is taken on the portfolio which could result in erosion of the principal amount invested. This implies that the investment has to be restricted to the specified instruments, issuers and has to be in line with the various norms.

- Liquidity – The investments have to be planned such that the desired quantum of funds could be withdrawn to meet any of the business requirements within a reasonable period of time.

- Return – Investments should be made with a view to optimize the post-tax return without making any compromise on the safety and liquidity. It is also to be ensured that at no point in time undue risk is taken on the portfolio in order to maximize the return.

Considering the above, generally, the investments can be done in various asset class such as:

- Bank Fixed Deposits – Low return high safety

- Debt Mutual Funds

- Corporate Fixed Deposits – Good return in long horizon, safe if put in good credit FDs (eg. AAA rated)

- Bonds – Good return in long horizon, safe if put in good credit FDs (eg. AAA rated)

Debt Mutual Funds

In the Indian context, discussion of Debt mutual funds is necessary since, many finance professionals are not aware of the nitty gritty of this sector. Depending on the horizon and the duration of the scheme, the schemes can be broadly divided as follows:

- Overnight funds – 1-day maturity papers – can be used to park idle funds over weekends

- Liquid funds – upto 3 months

- Ultra-short term – 3–6 months
- Money Market – upto 1 year
- Short duration funds – 1–3 years

There are two modes in which the money can be invested in the same scheme of a particular AMC (Asset Management Company) eg. HDFC Mutual Fund:

- Direct

If the investment is done through Direct route, the return on the investment is more by 0.05% to 0.35% depending on the expense ratio of various funds,

- Regular In case of regular, the distribution/broker under whose code one invests gets a commission from the AMC, hence the return on Investment is lower by 5bps – 35 bps as mentioned above.

Practically, the advisors/distributors (ARN code holders), either charge an advisory fee and invests the money on the direct code, or else, agree on a split of direct and regular without an advisory fee, which is a win-win for both the company as well as the advisor.

Let's take an example, if a company has raised $100M i.e. INR 700 crores apx. and wants to park the funds in various different asset classes. The first and the foremost thing that should be done is to estimate the cash burn of the company:

COMPANY'S CASH FLOW PLAN

Particulars	Amount (Crores)	Remarks
Collection(s)	4	Monthly
Expenditure(s)	-24	Monthly
Operation Cash Burn	-20	Monthly

*There is an acquisition planned in next 6 months, with an expected outflow to the tune of Rs. 210 Crores

Treasury Plan	Amount	Remarks
Cash available	**700**	Funds raised
Acquisition	-210	To be parked in Money Market/Callable FD
Exigency fund	-20	To be parked in Liquid Funds
Balance	**470**	
Monthly Burn	20	
Runway (Months)	23.5	

Quarterly bucketing:

Q1	60	To be parked in Liquid Funds/FD
Q2	60	To be parked in Ultra ST Funds
Q3	60	To be parked in Money Market
Q4	60	To be parked in Money Market
> 1 year	230	To be parked in Corporate FD – AAA rated/ Bank FD/Short Duration funds
> 2 year	Nil	

Let's assume the above investment of approx. 700 crores is done through direct and not the regular mode, a company can generate an extra return of Rs. 1 Crore (INR 10 Million) even if we assume a difference of 0.15% (15 bps) in return, which is quite significant.

b. **Tax planning & company law compliance** – Hope the taxman and the corporate law do not come hounding you. Typically, startups do not run into these issues in the initial years of operations. However, after three to four years, the past shortcomings are brought into the picture by the IT officials. Thus, it is amply important to plan for scrutiny assessments well in advance.

c. **IP valuation & TP study finance control** – Intellectual Property (IP) is a much-talked-about affair today. The IP of the business, ownership and the substance are the basis for taxation and revenue for the ex-chequer. It is vital to articulatethe clear understanding of the business, be aware of the advertisement campaigns/ announcements and make sure that the propagandas are in sync with the legal requirement.

d. **Revenue forecasts, expense monitoring, budgeting and variance analysis** – The investors are always interested in looking forward to forecasts, budgets and variances, if any. To present something and deliver it is a big challenge. The idea is to 'promise less and deliver more.'

e. **Pricing** – with application of unit economics, one can always work the right pricing of a product or a service. It is pertinent to note that, unit economics as the process through which pricing can be worked out is based on costing, however, other factors are equally important to be kept in mind like benchmarking of the pricing of similar products in the market.

f. **Legal contract review & contract management** – Contracts are not the sole responsibility of the legal team. The financial jargons, terms and the negotiation need to be taken care of from the business, finance and taxation point of view.

g. **Accounting policies, AR and AP; financial statements & audit** – Last but not the least, these account for the base of all the above pointers. If the recording and presentation of the transactions are correct from the very inception, the rest falls in place.

Org Structure - Finance

Broadly, to ensure the above, the finance function can be divided as follows:

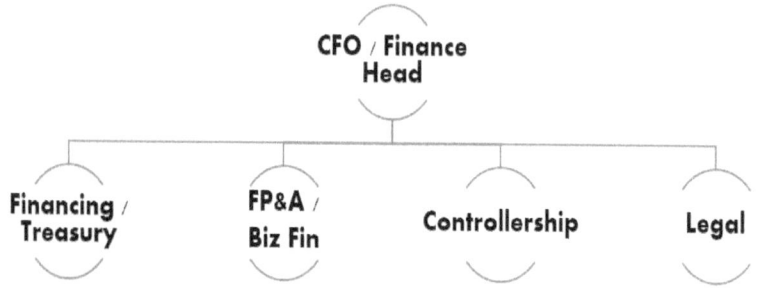

Financing (Fund Raising)/Treasury

- Debt/Equity

- Structured Debt

- Quasi – Instruments

- Investments

FP&A/Business Finance (Biz. Fin.)

- AOP (Annual Operating Plan)

- Budgeting

- Analysis

- Reporting (MIS)

- Pricing

Controllership

- Accounting

- Direct Tax – Income Tax

- Indirect Tax – GST

- Company Law

- FEMA

- Commercial Laws

Legal

- Agreements

- Contract Management

Depending on the level of the firm and the volume and scale of business, the finance team should be structured as above with a CFO/Finance head taking complete responsibility of all the sub-functions above. Some of the functions/duties may be overlapping considering the size and nature of operations, hence, it's wise to plan well to save costs

Excel skills

Spreadsheets are a must for any finance function to thrive and is indispensable. Infact, not only for finance, generally, spreadsheets are a very important tool to manage things well and must be taken seriously. If one is not very comfortable with the same, it is advisable to practise or as well train oneself if need be. These tools help finance, and accounting professionals create reports, analyse data, and prepare financial strategies. The Management Information system (MIS), Data book, financial models etc. are all built using MS Excel or the equivalent.

Some of the Key features and useful shortcuts in MS-Excel are:

Pivot Tables – A pivot table is a table of statistics that summarizes the data from a database. This summary might include sums, averages, or other statistics, which the pivot table groups together in a meaningful way.

VLOOKUP – This is a function to look up and retrieve data from a specific column in a table. It supports approximate and exact matching. The "V" stands for "vertical". Lookup values must appear in the first column of the table, with lookup columns to the right. Similarly, Hlookup looks for data in a horizontal row. [Do search for a new add-in called "Fuzzy Lookup"]

Filtering and Sorting – This function filters a range of data based on supplied criteria and extracts matching records. The sort function can sort the data in desired way e.g. Highest to lowest, alphabetically.

Offset – This function returns a reference to a range constructed inparts: a starting point, a row and a column offset, and also height and width in rows and columns. Offset is handy in formulas that dynamically average or sum "last n number of values".

Chapter 6

Culture vis-à-vis Finance

As discussed in the last chapter, there are various objective of the finance function. However, it is important to discuss the role of a Finance head or a CFO. Is it cost optimization, revenue generation, compliance management, managing Investors' expectations or pure business planning? No rewards for guessing it right. Yes, it is striving to achieve all of these, amid a bigger challenge of striking the right balance.

More often than not, all these objectives are contradicting; overlapping in nature and pose a bigger challenge for any finance leader in an organization, especially in case of Startups.

India is currently witnessing a phenomenal growth in terms of next-gen entrepreneurs, the capital availability/inflow and opportunities, which is creating more jobs and adding value to the economy. The bright minds of the country and the innovative approaches are trying to solve big problems for the countrymen; sometimes as laymen we don't even realize it to be a problem since we are so used to adjusting to our environment. Having worked with or advised both large corporates as well as the startups, one question that struck me was, what is better for a person who wants to make a career in finance? There are various factors to the same, viz. career, societal, innovation, satisfaction etc. In my view, from a career and other qualitative angle, one may get more learning in a startup environment rather than a big corporate.

However, there is a stark difference between a large corporate and a small company or a startup, when it comes to managing business and driving profits. Ironically, it is very interesting to note that in a large corporate, established systems and policies seem to be a bottleneck to decision making and growth in the initial phases, but later those very policies and principles help the company maintain the quality and give a long term fundamental growth. On the other hand, in case of startups, the teams start with super enthusiasm, agile mode with frequent scrums, quick decision making butunfortunately later bear the burn which in turn affects the whole organization due to failure of systems and policies. We have many live examples of improper utilization of VC/PE funds and mass layoffs in some well-known startups. Hence, the ask for striking a right balance, even in a startup, especially from a finance perspective.

While business development, technology, growth and marketing are vital & critical for any startup, so are other aspects of optimizing costs, driving growth and managing the Investors. Unfortunately, most of the functional heads perceive the finance team to be a roadblock to the growth and an unwanted; unnecessary policy makers, without understanding the nuances of business. However, this is not true, finance plays a strategic role in helping the business grow, hence a very judicious role of managing different stakeholder's expectation, keeping everyone happy and simultaneously ensuring all the compliance are in place. This thin line of difference is a tough task to be achieved. Thus, the question is 'How does one strike the right balance'?

The primary object is culture of the organization i.e. to understand that every function is equally indispensable for the growth of the company. "Every brick thinks that the wall is intact only because of it". The first step should be to keep the functional leaders aligned to the common goal and appreciate each other's effort. It may be done through cross learning presentations; scrum meetings, all-hands meet for teams as well as the company. As soon as the members start empathizing with each other's work, it becomes very easy to implement the policies and practices which would help the company grow with proper controls and checks as well adhere to the law of the land.

Followed by this, right and timely communication from the leadership team is imperative to give a sense of belonging to the employees and a feeling of ownership. These two steps will set the culture right and the rest will follow suit. Then, as a finance leader, it would be very easy to achieve the varied targets and expectations. Optimizing costs can be achieved through various measure like budgeting, functional revenue targets, measurable business metrics and cutting down unnecessary costs. Legal and taxation compliance can be easily complied with proper accounting systems in place with checks and control points month on month or even more frequently. Right data points, play a pivotal role in Investor reporting, managing finance, cash flows and returns. If different functions support and understand the relevance of these factors, it becomes easier for a finance head to implement policies, through which other functions benefit indirectly.

When the culture is set right and different teams work well with each other, the attrition in the company stays low resulting in better productivity and lowering the cost since hiring & firing is a costly affair and is a silent killer.

Finance plays a strategic role in terms of generating revenue through cost accounting, setting the right pricing of products or services, negotiation of deals & contracts. Once the above fragments are achieved, the Investor management becomes a cakewalk with proper reporting and growth. Do not forget to set the culture right before implementing policies.

Chapter 7

Startup India (Government's Initiative)

Startup India program started on 16th January 2016, is a flagship initiative of the Government of India, intended to catalyse startup culture and build a strong and inclusive ecosystem for innovation and entrepreneurship in India. It has rolled out many programs with an objective of supporting entrepreneurs, building a robust startup ecosystem and transforming India into a country of job creators instead of job seekers. These programs are managed by a dedicated Startup India Team, which reports to the Department for Industrial Policy and Promotion (DPIIT) under the Government of India.

There are various benefits for startups which can be availed through the portal such as:

a. DPIIT Registration

b. Various Government scheme for startups

c. Startup policies for states

d. Provision of services as an enabler in various fields.

The most beneficial being registration as a startup under DPIIT. Under the Startup India initiative, eligible companies can get recognized as startups by DPIIT, which gives them access to various tax benefits, easier compliance, Intellectual Property rights (IPR) and more.

To be eligible as a startup under DPIIT, a company must meet the following criteria:

- **Type** – The entity should be registered as a Private Limited **Company**, a registered **partnership** firm or a Limited Liability partnership **(LLP)**.

- **Age** – The entity should **not** be in existence and operations

- **exceeding 10 years** from the date of Incorporation.

- **Annual Turnover** – The turnover of the entity should **not exceed Rs. 100 crores** in any of the financial year since in-corporation.

- **Originality** – The entity should not have been formed by splitting up or reconstructing an already existing business.

- **Innovative and Scalable** – the entity should work towards development or improvement of a product, process or service and/ or have scalable business model with high potential for creation of wealth & employment.

Once the startup is eligible as per the above definition, it can register itself in the portal www.startupindia.gov.in, get recognized and avail hosts of benefits as follows. The registration process is very simple and is a matter of few minutes.

- **Labour law** – Startups can self-certify compliance under 6 labour laws and 3 environmental laws through a simple online procedure.

  - In case of labour laws, no inspections will be conducted for a period of 5 years unless there is a credible and verifiable written complaint filed for violation approved by atleast one level senior to the inspecting officer.

  - In case of environmental laws, startups which fall under the 'white category' (as defined by the Central Pollution Control Board (CPCB)) would be able to self-certify compliance and only random checks would be carried out in such cases A separate registration for the same need to be undertaken at https://shramsuvidha.gov.in/startUp.action

- **Intellectual property (Patent and Trademark)** – Patent application is a long-drawn process and is generally time consuming. For Startups, who innovate always wish to get their ideas patented. Under the program, the patent applications shall be fast tracked for examination, facilitators would be provided to assist in filing of IP applications by the government empanelled by the Controller General of Patents, Designs and Trademarks (CGPDTM) free of cost. The startups need to incur the statutory fees only. Further, the government provides 80% rebate on the patent filing fee.

- **Income Tax Exemption (S.80IAC of the Income Tax Act, 1961)** – Eligible startups are exempted from paying income tax for 3 consecutive financial years out of their first 10 (ten) years since incorporation.

  - The eligibility to avail this benefit are that the startup should be DPIIT recognised.

  - The entity should be a private limited company or an LLP

  - It should be incorporated after 1st April 2016

To avail the tax exemption, the startup should be recognized by DPIIT post registration under startup India by filling up the 80IAC exemption application along with few documents like MOA, Board resolution, Annual accounts and income tax return for last 3 financial years.

On verification of the eligibility, documents and ensuring that the startup is innovative and scalable, the DPIIT shall issue a exemption certificate, which can be used to avail the income tax exemption.

- **Easy Winding up of company** – The closure or winding up of a company is a cumbersome process and time consuming. Entrepreneurs loose money when capital gets blocked and hampers the flexibility of trying and failing. To address the same, Startup India makes it easier to wind up operations and allow founders to reallocate capital and resources to more productive avenues faster. The process is faster, simpler and quicker under the new law named The Insolvency and Bankruptcy code, 2016 (IBC 2016).

- **Easier Public procurement Norms** – To give access to a larger market, the government and state-owned purchases ofgoods and services from the private sector has been made easier in terms of exemptions and opportunities like:

  - Listing of products in the Government e Marketplace (GeM),an online procurement platform and the largest marketplace for Government Departments to procure products and services.

  - Exemption from the requirement of having prior experience/ turnover for the manufacturing sector.

  - EMD Exemption – DPIIT recognised startups have been exempted from submitting Earnest Money Deposit (EMD) or bid security while filling government tenders.

The famous idiom in Hindi:

गिरते हैं शहसवार ही मैदान-ए-जंिमें ।
वो गतफ़्ल क्या गिरे िजो घुटनों के बल चले ।

The english translation of the above is, the horse-rider falls from his horse in the war, the coward who crawls and does not have the courage to ride will never fall from the horse.

This means the person who has the courage to take risks and bold steps, who has the courage to take a bumpy ride in difficult circumstances, only those brave souls know the power of fulfilment, the joy of achievement. On the other hand, who is not courageous enough to even walk – leave aside riding a horse – will never experience the sense of accomplishment.

Wish you a lot of failures, falls and rises!

'The greatest glory of living lies not in never falling, but in rising every time you fall'

– Nelson Mandela

Annexures

Cap Table: Cap Table Sample Private Limited

Fully Diluted Cap Table as at 31-Dec-2019

Shareholders	Residential Status	Equity Shares	(On an As If Converted Basis)					(on a Fully Diluted Basis)	
			Series A CCPS	Series A1 CCPS	Series B CCPS	Series C CCPS	Series C1 CCPS	Total Shareholding	% Shareholding
Promoter 1	India	5,00,000	-	-	-	-	-	5,00,000	12.75%
Promoter 2	India	5,00,000	-	-	-	-	-	5,00,000	12.75%
Employee Shareholder	India	2,000	-	-	-	-	-	2,000	0.05%
ESOP Pool	NA	1,00,000	-	-	-	-	-	1,00,000	2.55%
MSOP Pool	NA	2,00,000	-	-	-	-	-	2,00,000	5.10%
Investor 1	Cayman Islands	100	-	1,20,000	2,00,000	7,00,000	-	10,20,100	26.01%
Investor 2	Singapore	100	5,00,000	-	-	200000	-	7,00,100	17.85%
Investor 3	Mauritius	100	-	-	-	7,00,000	1,00,000	8,00,100	20.40%
Angel Investor 1	India	70,000	-	-	-	-		70,000	1.78%
Angel Investor 2	Singapore	30,000	-	-	-	-	-	30,000	0.76%
Total		14,02,300	5,00,000	1,20,000	2,00,000	16,00,000	1,00,000	39,22,300	100.00%

Note: The actual number of Series A1 CCPS issued by the Company to Investor 1 is 1,00,000. Conversion Ratio 1:1.2

Equity TS

MEMORANDUM OF TERMS FOR PURCHASE OF PREFERRED SHARES OF XYZ PVT. LTD.

November 1, 2019

This memorandum summarizes the principal terms of the contemplated purchase of preferred shares of XYZ Pvt Ltd. This memorandum is for discussion purposes only and is not intended to be construed as a binding agreement. The completion of the transactions contemplated by this memorandum will be subject to, among other things, satisfactory completion of financial and legal due diligence by the Investors, as well as the completion of final documents acceptable to the Investors.

Offering Terms

Company:	XYZ Pvt Ltd, an Indian company.
Investors:	FGH Fund I Pte Ltd.
Total Investment Amount:	$80 million, of which the Investors shall fund $30 million.
Securities to be Issued:	Preferred shares (the "Shares").
Price:	Such price per Share as shall reflect a $200 million pre-money valuation of the Company. The Shares shall represent 20.12% of the post-money fully diluted capitalization of the Company (including all existing options and warrants and all shares reserved for issuance under the Company's stock option plan including those described below).

Continued...

Option Pool:	The Company shall increase its option pool prior to the closing so that the management team is granted new equity representing 3% of the Company's fully diluted capitalization post-closing.
Terms of Preferred Shares Dividends/Liquidation Preference Conversion/ Antidilution/Other Rights:	The Shares shall enjoy preferred rights with respect to dividends, liquidation preference, conversion, antidilution and other rights which are pari passu with the rights of the existing preferred shares.
Terms of Shareholder Agreements Shareholder Rights:	The Company shall amend its shareholders agreement to reflect the issuance of the Shares but otherwise the shareholders agreement shall retain its existing substantive provisions.

The parties hereto understand and acknowledge that this memorandum is for discussion purposes only and is not a legally binding agreement and that the failure to execute and deliver a definitive agreement shall impose no liability on the Investors. If the terms of this memorandum are acceptable to the Company, please so indicate on the enclosed copy of this memorandum and return it to the undersigned no later than July 5, 2019.

AGREED AND ACCEPTED:

XYZ Pvt Ltd.	FGH Fund I Pte Ltd
By: Name	**By: Name**
Title	**Title**

CP Confirmation & Subscription Notice

CP Completion Letter

[ON THE LETTERHEAD OF THE COMPANY]

To xx.xx. 2019
[Insert name of Investor]
[insert address]

Kind Attn: [insert name], [insert resignation]

Re: CP Confirmation Letter

Dear Sirs,

We refer to the Share Subscription Agreement dated **10 January** 2019 executed between **XYZ** I Pte Ltd., **AZP** AIF – I, **Onde** Trust, **Sample** Venture Debt Fund – I (together, "Investors"), the Company, **Founder 1** and **Founder 2** ("Agreement").

We hereby confirm, declare and certify pursuant to Clause **xx** (*CP Confirmation Letter*) of the Agreement, that as on the date hereof all conditions precedent as set out in Schedule **x** to the Agreement have been fulfilled to the satisfaction of each of the Investors.

We enclose herewith copies of relevant documents evidencing completion of the condition precedent.

Capitalized words and expressions used in this letter but not defined herein shall have the same meaning as assigned to them in the Agreement.

Yours sincerely,

_____

For and on behalf of HJK PRIVATE LIMITED

Name:

Designation: Director

_____

Subscription Notice

[ON THE LETTERHEAD OF THE COMPANY]

[xx.xx.] 2019

To,

Each Investor/Subscriber

Kind Attention: Mr. X/Board of Directors
Ladies and Gentlemen:

Request for Subscription of 534,352 Series D CCCPS

1. Please refer to the Share Subscription Agreement (**Subscription Agreement**), dated xx December 2019, amongst, *inter alia*, FGH Private Limited (**Company**), ONF Fund II Pte Ltd, Indo Investment VI (Mauritius) Ltd, Apple Capital Limited. Terms defined in the Subscription Agreement, including terms defined by reference to any other Transaction Document (as defined in the Subscription Agreement), have their defined meanings wherever used in this request.

2. In accordance with the provisions of the Subscription Agreement and the enclosed resolution of the Company's board of directors and shareholders, the Company requests the subscription of 534,352 Series D CCCPS for an aggregate consideration equal to INR 10,06,23,206. Therefore, the Company requests Blue Wolf Capital Limited to pay INR 10,06,23,206 on the Closing Date to:

Bank name	RTY Bank
Bank address	120, Hosur Road, Bengaluru, Karnataka 5600XX
SWIFT	XXXXXXXXXX
Beneficiary name	FGH Private Limited – Capital Account
Account number	40XXXXXXX385
IFSC Code	CXXXXXXX56

3. The Closing Date for the subscription contemplated by this Subscription Notice shall be [xx.xx] 2019.

4. The CP Confirmation Letter is enclosed in accordance with Clause 2.3 of the Subscription Agreement.

5. The above certifications are effective as of the date of this Subscription Notice and shall continue to be effective as of the Closing Date set out in paragraph 3 (as if made by reference to such date). If any such certification is no longer valid as of or prior to that Closing Date, the Company undertakes to promptly notify [Investor] by facsimile.

Yours faithfully,

By _____

Authorized Representative

Enclosures:	Resolution of the Company's board of directors and shareholders
	CP Confirmation Letter

DOA

Investor Deed of Adherence

THIS INVESTOR DEED OF ADHERENCE ("Deed") is made on the _____ day of _____, 2019

BY:

HJK PRIVATE LIMITED, a company incorporated under the laws of India and having its registered office at [xxx[(hereinafter referred to as "Company"), which expression shall, unless repugnant to the context or meaning thereof, be deemed to mean and include its successors and permitted assigns);

Mr. XYZ [New Shareholder], an Individual and having its residence at 808, Cee Suite, Shiv Mandir Estate, Sour Road, Mumbai 400 0XX (hereinafter referred to as "New Shareholder", which expression shall, unless repugnant to the context or meaning thereof, be deemed to mean and include its successors and permitted assigns);

Mr. PQR [Selling Shareholder], an Individual and having its residence at 607, Cee Suite, Shiv Mandir Estate, Hour Road, Mumbai 400 1XX (hereinafter referred to as "Selling Shareholder", which expression shall, unless repugnant to the context or meaning thereof, be deemed to mean and include its successors and permitted assigns);

WHEREAS

A. The New Shareholder has purchased [number and description] shares of [INR xxxx] each in the Company from the Selling shareholder.

B. This Deed is entered into pursuant to an agreement (the "Shareholders' Agreement") dated [ ], made between [names of parties to the SHA]

NOW, THEREFORE, THIS DEED WITNESSETH AS FOLLOWS:

1. The New Shareholder confirms that he has received a copy of the Shareholder's agreement and undertakes to be bound by all its terms that are capable of applying to him with effect from the date on which he is registered as a shareholder in the books of the Company.

2. Nothing in this deed shall release the Transferor of shares in the Company to the New Shareholder from any liability in respect of any obligations under the Shareholders' agreement which were due to be performed by him before the date of this deed.

3. Representations and Warranties

    The Investor represents and warrants to the Original Parties that the Investor is a resident of India and is subject to tax in India and that its execution of this Deed (i) has been duly authorized and that such execution or compliance with its terms shall not now, or at any time in the future, conflict with or result in a breach of any of the terms, conditions or provisions of, or constitute a default or require any consent under, any agreement or other instrument they have executed or by which they are bound, or violate any of the terms and provisions of any statutory documents or any judgment, decree or order or any statute, rule or regulation applicable to it; (ii) is incompliance with applicable Indian Laws.

4. Governing Law and Jurisdiction

    This Deed shall be governed in all respects by the laws of India and subject to the exclusive jurisdiction to the courts in Mumbai, India.

5. Definitions

Terms used but not defined herein shall have the meanings assigned to them in the Shareholders' Agreement.

IN WITNESS WHEREOF, the Original Parties and the Investor have entered into this Deed the day and year first above written in _____, 2019.

Signed and delivered for and on behalf of :

HKJ Pvt. Ltd.	Selling Shareholder	New Shareholder
By:	By:	By:
Title	Title	Title

Debt TS

Debt Term Sheet (Non-NCD)

Term Sheet

XYZ Pvt. Ltd. November 3, 2019
#303, 8th Floor, Main Rd,
Sector 9, Monte Layout,
Bangalore, Karnataka, India

Dear Ken,

The purpose of this letter is to outline the terms and conditions that Venture Debt Capital India Pvt. Ltd. ("Venture Debt") is willing to consider regarding financing for you ("the Company" or "Borrower"). This letter is for discussion purposes only. It is not, in any manner, to be construed as a commitment or agreement on the part of Venture Debt to provide this financing, which is subject to the satisfactory conclusion of our credit approval process.

TERMS AND CONDITIONS – TERM LOAN FACILITY

Facility:	Fixed Rate Rupee Term Loan
Facility Amount and availability:	Rs. 300,000,000 (Rupees Three Hundred Million Only), tranched as follows:
	Tranche I: Rs. 150,000,000/- Tranche II: Rs. 150,000,000/-

Facility:	Fixed Rate Rupee Term Loan
Availability:	Tranche I: November15, 2019 Tranche II: June 15, 2020 contingent on the company achieving 80% of their submitted plan on key financial metrics.
Purpose:	General Corporate Purposes
Interest Rate:	15.50% p.a.
Interest Payable:	Payable monthly
Maturity:	August 31, 2022 for both the tranches.
Principal Repayment:	Each Advance will be amortized on a monthly basis starting from July 1, 2020 for Tranche I and October 1, 2020 for Tranche II.
Upfront loan Fee:	1% of the Facility Amount exclusive of taxes, payable upfront at the time of closing of the Facility
Right to subscribe:	On closing, The Borrower shall grant Venture Debt the right to purchase the Borrower's Preferred Shares equal to the following: • For Tranche I: Rs. 15,000,000 divided by price per share that is 15–20% discount to the next financing round price i.e. Series D round provided the same is closed by December 2020. • For Tranche II: Rs. 15,000,000 shall be price per share of the Series D round provided the same is closed by December 2020. This Right can be exercised at any time over a period of eight years from the date of issuance. Anti-Dilution and Liquidation Preference Rights provided to the same class of shareholders will apply. The right granted hereunder shall survive the termination of the loan Agreement.

Facility:	Fixed Rate Rupee Term Loan
Right to Invest:	The Borrower shall grant Venture Debt or its affiliates a right (but not an obligation) to invest up to USD 3 Million in the Borrower's Subsequent Financing rounds on the same terms, conditions and pricing offered to its investors in those rounds. The right granted hereunder shall survive the termination of the loan Agreement.
Prepayment:	Prepayment is not permitted till Mar 31, 2021. Prepayment is thereafter permitted, with a prepayment penalty equal to 1% of the outstanding loan amount.
Default/Penal Interest:	Amounts unpaid on due date will attract additional interest at 1.00% per month, compounded annually.
Material Adverse Change:	In the opinion of Venture Debt (i) a material impairment in the perfection of Venture Debt's Lien in the collateral or in the value of such collateral (ii) a material adverse change in the business, operations or condition (financial or otherwise) of Borrower (iii) a material impairment of the prospect of repayment of any portion of the obligations. MAC to be an event of default.
Security:	Exclusive first charge by way of hypothecation on all the fixed, current and non-current assets (including IP) of the Company. Form CHG – 1 shall be filed with the Registrar of Companies within 10 days of the disbursement of the Facility.
Documentation:	As prescribed by Venture Debt including but not limited to: <ul><li>Loan & Security Agreement</li><li>Board Resolution for availing the facilities from Venture Debt along with signature verification of the authorized signatories</li><li>Certified True copies of the Company's MOA and AOA</li><li>Request Letter for the Facility</li></ul>

Facility:	Fixed Rate Rupee Term Loan
Reporting:	• Consolidated monthly and year-till-date financial statements (P&L, Balance Sheet, and Cash Flow) and operating metrics of Borrower and for each operating entity within 30 days of month end; • Annual consolidated audited financial statements of the Borrower within 180 days of year-end, certified by independent certified public accountants acceptable to Venture Debt;
	• Annual operating budgets and projections within 45 days of financial year end; and • Details of existing borrowing limits and outstanding within 30 days of Month-end • Cash position (Encumbered and Free Cash) of the Borrower and each operating entity at the end of every month within 10 days of the end of every month.
Expenses:	Borrower agrees to pay all costs, fees and expenses incurred by the Lender in connection with the loan documentation.
Marketing:	Borrower agrees to Venture Debt using the Company's logo to highlight the relationship in Venture Debt's Marketing materials.
Confidentiality:	This Term Sheet is confidential, and contents of this letter may not be disclosed by the Company without Venture Debt's prior written consent.

If the basic terms and conditions described above are acceptable, please remit to us a sum of Rs. 300,000 ("Advance against Loan Fee") together with a signed copy of this on or before February 6, 2019.

If the proposed loan transaction closes, Venture Debt will apply the Advance toward its Costs. If Venture Debt declines to proceed with the loan transaction, Venture Debt will return the Deposit less Costs incurred by Venture Debt (including fees of attorneys and examiners). If Venture Debt approves the loan transaction, but the loan transaction does not close (other than as a result of a breach by Venture Debt of its commitment), Venture Debt shall retain the entire Advance.

This Term Sheet is intended for your guidance and information only and does not constitute an offer commitment or agreement to enter into a loan transaction. The signature by the Borrower on this Term Sheet shall not cause Venture Debt to be committed to enter into a loan transaction with the Borrower. Any legal relationship will be evidenced by definitive documentation, which will be prepared following your acceptance of the offer and satisfactory conclusion of our credit approval process.

Sincerely,

Jhon Day	Jhonny Daddy Director
Chief Executive Officer, India Venture Debt Capital India Pvt. Ltd.	Venture Debt Capital India Pvt. Ltd.

AGREED & ACCEPTED, this _____ day of _____, 2019.

By: Sample Com Private Limited

Name: _____

Title: _____

Debt Term Sheet (NCD)

Term Sheet

01 Feb 2019

To,

Sampling Com Private Limited,
Gali No.2, Mumbai.

Dear Zen,

This term sheet outlines the indicative terms and conditions that VenDee Capital India Fund I ("Investor"), represented by its investment manager VenDee Capital Advisors LLP ("Investment Manager") is willing to consider regarding the facility proposed to be availed by Sampling Com Private Limited ("**Company**", "**Sampling**") on mutually agreed terms ("**Term Sheet**"). The Term Sheet is non-binding in nature other than the provisions described under the heads Expenses, Governing Law and Confidentiality and is intended for your guidance and information only.

No.	Terms	Particulars
1.	**Borrower**	Sampling Com Private Limited
2.	**Purpose**	General Corporate Purpose
3.	**Availability**	Facility to be available in 2 tranches • Tranche I – upto February 28, 2019 • Tranche II – upto May 31, 2019
4.	**Instruments**	(a) Unlisted, secured and redeemable Non-Convertible Debenture ("**NCDs**") (b) Partly paid-up Compulsorily Convertible Preference Shares ("**CCPS**")

No.	Terms	Particulars
5.	**Debt Amount**	Total amount of INR 50,00,00,000 (Rupees Fifty Crore only) through the issue of 1,500 NCDs, each with a face value of INR 100,000 (Rupees One Lakh Only) in two tranches as below • Tranche I – INR 25,00,00,000 (Rupees Twenty-Five Crore Only) • Tranche II – INR 25,00,00,000 (Rupees Twenty-five Crore Only)
6.	**Equity Amount**	(a) INR 1,50,00,000 (Rupees One Crore Fifty Lakh only) through the issue of applicable number of CCPS at the Subscription Price (Price per share as determined in the Series A round). Each CCPS shall be partly paid up to the extent of INR 1. The CCPS will be issued on the closure of debt documentation. Investor will have the option, exercisable at its sole discretion, to fully pay up the CCPS at any time up to 8 years from date of allotment. CCPS shall have similar rights as given to holders of the Series B round.
7.	**Right to Invest**	Investor shall have unfettered right (but not the obligation) to subscribe to the share capital of the Company up to an amount equal to INR 14,00,00,000 (Rupees Fourteen Crore) in a future round of investment on the terms similar to those offered to the other investors participating in a future round of investment. The right so granted shall survive up to the subsequent round of investment. The right shall survive beyond the maturity of the NCD, where the subsequent round of investment has not occurred prior to maturity. Should the Investor not opt to exercise the right in the subsequent round of investment, the right shall lapse.

No.	Terms	Particulars
8.	Tenor	The NCD shall mature on 1st September 2021
9.	Interest Rate	Fixed rate of 14.00% per annum, payable monthly
10.	Additional Coupon	Non-refundable additional coupon of 1% of the Total Debt Amount, exclusive of all applicable taxes and payable upfront at the time of investment of Tranche I Debt Amount.
11.	Moratorium	The Debt Amount shall start amortizing on a monthly basis starting September 2019
12.	Principal Repayment	Amortized on a monthly basis in 25 equal instalments commencing 1st September 2019. Installments shall be payable on the 1st day of the month.
13.	Prepayment	Prepayment shall not be permitted before 12 months. Thereafter, prepayment shall be permitted subject to payment of a prepayment penalty as below • >12 months to 18 months – 2.5% of the outstanding Debt Amount • >18 months to 24 months – 2.0% of the outstanding Debt Amount • > 24 months – 1% of the outstanding Debt Amount
14.	Security	Exclusive hypothecation over all fixed and current assets of the Company, both present and future.

No.	Terms	Particulars
15.	Material Adverse Change ('MAC')	"Material Adverse Change" means an event or circumstance which has or could reasonably be expected to have, in the sole opinion of the Majority Debenture Holders, a material adverse effect on: (i) the condition (financial or otherwise), operations, business or assets of the Company, which adversely impacts the ability of the Company to meet its payment obligations under the Transaction Documents; or (ii) the validity or enforceability of the Security/ Security Interest or part thereof created in relation to the NCD
16.	Events of Default (EOD) and Penal Interest.	EOD and its consequences shall be detailed in the Transaction Documents. Upon the occurrence of an EOD, additional interest at the rate of 1% per month will be applicable from the date of occurrence of the EOD till the date it is cured.
17.	Other Key Terms	The Transaction Documents shall contain customary provisions relating to: (a) manner, terms and conditions for issuance of the Instruments, including the conditions precedent and conditions subsequent; (b) covenants, representations and warranties by the Company and/or the [Promoters]; (c) consequent indemnity obligations of the Company and/or the [Promoters]; and (d) other terms auxiliary to venture debt.

No.	Terms	Particulars
18.	**Due Diligence**	The Investor shall have the right to carry out legal, financial, business, tax and commercial due diligence on the Company and its business and operations prior to entering into any of the transactions contemplated herein.
19.	**Reporting**	As may be prescribed by the Investor and Debenture Trustee including, but not limited to: (a) Monthly financial statements within 30 days of month end; (b) Monthly operating metrics within 30 days of month end; (c) Annual audited financial statement within 180 days of year end; (d) Annual business projections within 45 days of year end; and (e) Other information metrics as may be requested by the Investor (f) Other reporting as may be requested by the Investor and Debenture Trustee.
20.	**Expenses**	The Company shall pay all costs, fees and expenses incurred by the Investor and Debenture Trustee in relation to the Transaction Documents, due diligence, creation of Security and remuneration of Debenture Trustee.
21.	**Confidentiality**	The term sheet is confidential and contents of this letter may not be disclosed by the Company without Investor's prior written consent.
22.	**Governing Law and Jurisdiction**	This Term Sheet shall be governed in accordance with Indian Law. Courts at Delhi alone shall have the exclusive jurisdiction to entertain and try and disputes arising thereof.

No.	Terms	Particulars
23.	**Transaction Documents**	As prescribed by Investor, including but not limited to: • Securities Subscription Agreement • Debenture Trust Deed • Deed of Hypothecation • Debenture Trustee Agreement
24.	**Marketing**	The Company agrees to permit the Investor to use its logo and brand name for the Investor's marketing

If the terms and conditions described above are acceptable, please remit to the Investor an advance against the Additional Coupon ofINR 300,000 (Rupees Three Lakh Only) exclusive of all applicable taxes ("**Advance**") together with a signed copy of this Term Sheet within 7 days from the date of this Term Sheet.

Post receipt of the Advance, if the Investor declines to proceed with the transaction, the entire advance would be refunded to the Company. However, if the Company declines to proceeds with the transaction, the advance net of expenses would be refunded to the Company.

Sincerely,

For VenDee Capital acting through its Investment Manager VenDee Capital Advisors LLP

Signature: Signature:
Name: Champak Sharzie   Name: Mansu Samara
Designation: Partner   Designation: Senior Principal

Agreed & accepted, on the _____ day of _____, 2019

By Sampling Com Private Limited

Signature:
Name:
Designation:

Taxation

Taxation of ESOPs

Typically, the life cycle of ESOPs has three stages – vesting period, exercise i.e. conversion of options to shares and Sale of shares.

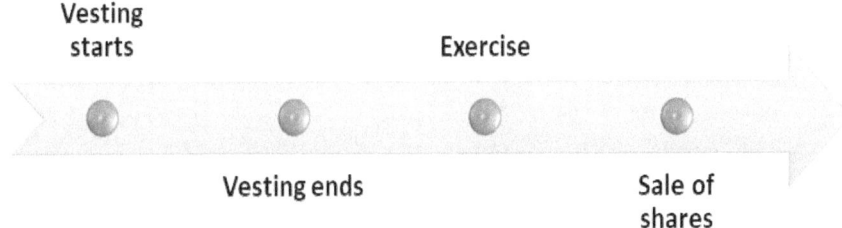

The employee stock options are taxed in a peculiar way in India in two stages. The employee pays taxes at the time of:

a. Exercise of options

    Tax is paid by the employee on the fair value of shares on the date of exercise reduced by the exercise price. This fair value becomes the cost for the employee here onwards.

b. Sale of shares

    Tax is paid by the employee on the sale value less the cost i.e. FV at the time of exercise.

Example:

Number of options vested – 100
Face value per share – Rs. 10

Exercise price – Rs. 50

Fair value per share on the date of exercise – Rs. 90
Sale price per share after one year of exercise – Rs. 150

Taxability

a. On the date of exercise:

No. of shares × (FV – Exercise Price)
100 × (90 – 50) = 4,000

Rs. 4,000 shall become part of salary and applicable tax to be paid thereon.

Rs. 90 now becomes the cost per share for the employee.

b. On the date of sale:

No. of shares × (Sale Price – Cost)
100 × (150 – 90) = 6,000

Rs. 6,000 is taxed as a Capital gain and applicable tax to be paid thereon.

Total gain of Rs. 100 (150–50) per share is taxed in two stages as above.

It is interesting to note that at the first stage of exercise, the employee ends up shelling out tax from his pocket, without even making real money, since he has just converted his options into shares and pays tax on a notional gain, which is a negative cashflow. If the company does not do well in the future and he is unable to sell the shares, he ends up bearing a loss. This is a dampener for employees in the startup world. The same may still be considered to be fine for an employee of a listed company, since there is a ready market and the employees have a choice of selling their shares immediately after exercise, if they wish to. However, in case of startups, there is no choice left with the employees.

Note: Recently, in the budget 2020, the Government has tried to address this issue and proposed to give some breather in taxation at the time of exercise. The point of taxation for the exercise stage, has been deferred to the earliest of the following and shall no more be taxed at the time of exercise:

i.   Exit from the company

ii. Sale of shares

iii. 5 years from the date of exercise

The above means, if the shares are sold within 5 years of exercise and the employee is still working in the company, the taxation is in just one stage i.e. the sale of shares.

However, it may not be very fruitful for employees, who plan to exercise at the time of leaving the company or the companies which are not able to give a selling opportunity to the employees within 5 years of exercise.

Goods and Service Tax (GST)

There are three types of taxes under GST

Central GST (CGST); State GST (SGST); Integrated GST (IGST) Simply put CGST + SGST = IGST

In case of Intra state transactions i.e. within the same state, CGST and SGST is applicable whereas in case of Inter-state transactions i.e. between two states, IGST is applicable. Hence, One India One Tax. Irrespective of the place and destination of a business transaction, the tax rates are same.

The Tax rates under GST are 0%, 5%, 12%, 18% and 28%.

The rates for goods and services vary depending on the type of product or services. Mostly, the rate would fall under either of the tax rates except some special rates.

Tax Rates	Products
0%	Regular consumption including fresh fruits and vegetables, milk, butter milk, curd, natural honey, flour, besan, bread, all kinds of salt, jaggery, hulled cereal grains, fresh meat, fish, chicken, eggs etc.
0.25%	Cut and semi-polished stones are included under this tax slab.
5%	Household necessities such as edible oil, sugar, spices, tea, and coffee (except instant) are included. Coal, Mishti/Mithai (Indian Sweets) and Life-saving drugs are also covered under this GST slab.
12%	This includes computers and processed food
18%	Hair oil, toothpaste and soaps, capital goods and industrial intermediaries are covered in this slab.
28%	Luxury items such as small cars, consumer durables like AC and Refrigerators, premium cars, cigarettes and aerated drinks, High-end motorcycles are included here.

GST rate for services is 18% generally, however, some services may fall under other tax slabs.

Tax Rates	Products
0%	Chargeable services offered on Basic Savings Bank Deposit (BSBD) account opened under the Pradhan Mantri Jan Dhan Yojana, Hotel accommodation for transaction value per unit per day being Rs. 1000 or less etc.
5%	Renting a motor cab without fuel cost, Transport services in AC contract/stage or radio taxi, Print media ad space etc.
12%	IP rights on a temporary basis, Air travel excluding economy, Food/drinks at restaurants without AC/heating or liquor license etc.
18%	General Rate, whichever is not included under other tax slabs.
28%	Food/drinks at AC 5-star hotels, Race club services, Gambling

Note: The examples for GST rates mentioned above is not exhaustive and only indicative.

About the Author

CA. Rahul Saria

(Cofounder @Fincurious; All India Rankholder CA & CS; Business Leader 40 under 40 by ICAI & CNBC; TEDx speaker and Author of 2 books)

Rahul is a co-founder of **an Edtech Startup** - https://fincurious.com/ . He has served as CFO / head of finance for various global and Indian startups like Vedantu (Unicorn), Rentomojo (Fintech) and Near.com (Nasdaq Listed) in the past. He has extensive experience (14+ years) in fund raising (Debt & Equity ~ $200Mn+), finance controllership, FP&A, Business Finance & Treasury ($150Mn).

He holds a host of qualifications: Chartered Accountant (Fellow Member), Company Secretary, DISA, IFRS, Valuation, Blockchain Technology, PMLA, PGDBA (IMT-G), M&A (IIM-B); Financial Modelling (EY).

He was an **All-India Rank holder – AIR** 15th in CA Final, AIR 2nd in CA Inter, **AIR** 11th in CS Final and AIR 25th in CS Inter. He has been awarded **"CA Business Leader 40 under 40"** by ICAI and CNBC in 2023. Also awarded **"CA Professional Achiever – Services Sector 2016"** by ICAI. He has also been awarded 'RAJYA PURASKAR' by Governor of WB for excellence in Scouting & Service to mankind. He is also an author of two books on Startups – **Fincurious and Startup Finance 360.**

He is a veteran speaker and has also authored several articles. He has been recognized as National Level Faculty for GST, UAE VAT, GMCS and Orientation course by ICAI. He also deliberates on Startup Finance, Taxation, MS Excel, Soft Skills, Business Process at corporate forums.

A TEDx speaker at Christ University. He was also a board member of **Toastmasters International** District 92.

Linkedin Profile:

https://www.linkedin.com/in/ca-rahul-saria/

www.ingramcontent.com/pod-product-compliance
Lightning Source LLC
Chambersburg PA
CBHW021419210526
45463CB00001B/454